V.I.P.E.R. Improvement:

Fire/EMS Department

Leadership and Management

Dr. David Hupp

Published by: V.I.P.E.R. Improvement Publishing

Author: Dr. David Hupp

ISBN: 979-8-218-40335-5

Dedication

To my mother and father, for raising me.

To my wife Nancy, for believing in me.

To my daughter Autumn and stepson Ryan, for completing me.

And I heard the voice of the Lord saying, "Whom shall I send, and who will go for us?" Then I said, "Here I am! Send me."

Isaiah 6:8 (ESV)

Table of Contents

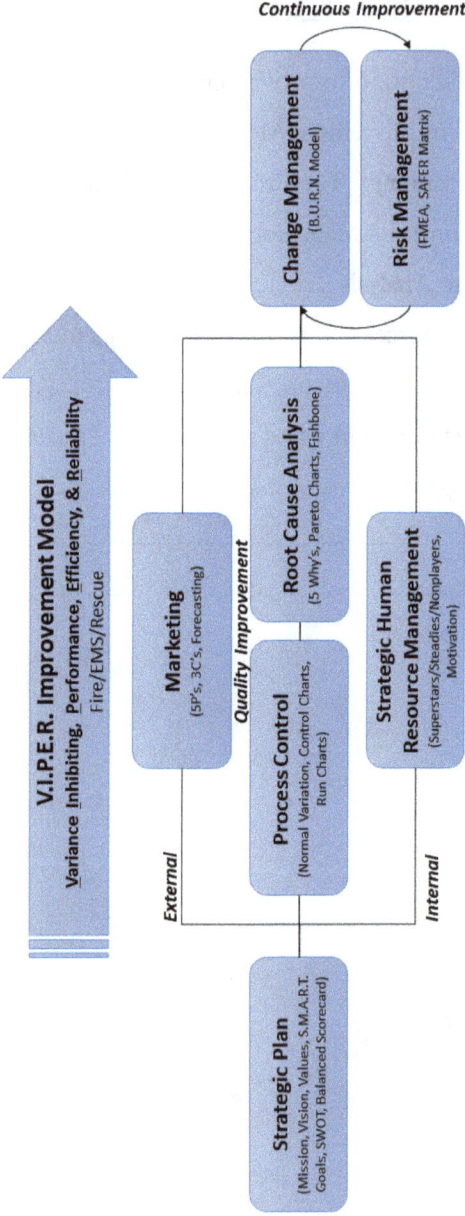

V.I.P.E.R. Improvement Model

Variance Inhibiting, Performance, Efficiency, & Reliability
Fire/EMS/Rescue

Continuous Improvement

Change Management	Risk Management
(B.U.R.N. Model)	(FMEA, SAFER Matrix)

Quality Improvement

Marketing
(5P's, 3C's, Forecasting)

Root Cause Analysis
(5 Why's, Pareto Charts, Fishbone)

Process Control
(Normal Variation, Control Charts, Run Charts)

Strategic Human Resource Management
(Superstars/Steadies/Nonplayers, Motivation)

External

Internal

Strategic Plan
(Mission, Vision, Values, S.M.A.R.T. Goals, SWOT, Balanced Scorecard)

Chapter 1: An Introduction to Improvement

You have just been elected as a new leader of your department (president, chief, board of director, officer). You are sitting at your first meeting and listening to the group discuss some pressing issues. About halfway through the discussion they all look to you and ask, "what do you want to do about this?" As a leader, you are expected to provide direction as others in the department are looking to you for answers. This can be dauting, even for seasoned veterans to leadership. But now you have been put on the spot. How do you respond? You could give your opinion based on your experience, which might be a good course of action. You were elected for this purpose after all. The downside is that your opinion is one of many, and there may be a perspective or solution that you haven't thought of yet. But to waiver too long can make you look indecisive, and may make you seem weak early on in your tenure (which can be difficult to come back from). So again, what do you do?

This situation is common and happens all the time. Essentially what it boils down to is problem solving. Tackling problems in a purposeful way is a cornerstone to leadership. The dilemma above can play out on the fireground as well, where competent and confident decision-making needs to occur as problems arise. The issue that many departments face today is that there is a lack of systematic problem solving. By this I mean there is a lack of structure to addressing problems in a routine fashion.

Quality Improvement: What is it?

This book uses the concept and mindset that improvements or changes within a department need to be *purposeful*. They need to be carried out in a thoughtful and strategic manner that draws on critical thinking tools. This idea is more commonly known as quality improvement.

Quality improvement is the enhancement of a process or outcome using tools and techniques within a system. When you want to improve something or change something for the better, tools and techniques are used within a system or framework that is backed by science, experts, and evidence. One can see quality improvement in everyday life. When someone wants to lose weight, they use quality improvement. The tools are diet and exercise; and the system is the regimen or schedule. If you want improve strength, weight training and supplements are the tools, and the type of workout and pre/post supplement schedule is the system. If one wants to improve their credit score, the tools are credit cards and making payments, but the system is understanding the percentage of the score that is impacted by length of credit history, amount owed, payment history, and other factors. It's critical to understand that in order to truly improve something one needs tools to help the improvement, the use of these tools within a system so one's work is synergistic and not working in opposition to each other, and that these are based and grounded in reliable science, expert consensus, and evidence. If a quality improvement mindset isn't used, then goals will ultimately not be reached. Weight loss will not occur or won't be sustained and come back, strength gains will be marginal or plateau, and credit scores might hit a frustrating ceiling. For fire/EMS departments, quality improvement can have infinite applications: developing a plan to increase recruitment, figuring out why lifetime members aren't as involved as they used to be, identifying how to roll out a new EMS protocol, figuring out where to invest efforts in fundraising . . . the sky is the limit for application.

Addressing problems in a structured fashion creates stability, which is the foundation that quality improvement is built upon. SOG's/SOP's and assignments are an example of addressing a situation in a structured fashion because it produces degrees of stability, predictability, and reliability on an incident. Deviations, or variance, from this structure leads to freelancing, which is a risk that the V.I.P.E.R. Improvement Model would constitute as an unstable condition or outlier (see Ch. 4). So, if a fire/EMS department wants to fix a process, or improve a result, they need to use quality improvement. This book proposes that the V.I.P.E.R.

Improvement Model is the best quality improvement model tailored specifically for fire/EMS use.

This book was undertaken to assist departments in purposefully tackling problems, which is unfortunately seldom seen due to a lack of resources for improvement dedicated to the fire and EMS industry. Consider the following macro-level problems facing volunteer firefighters today found in NFPA's US Fire Department Profile (Fahy et al., 2022):

- In 2020, fire department call volume has tripled since the 1980's (10,819,000 to 36,416,000).

- The number of volunteer firefighters is down 25% (1986: 808,200, 2020: 676,900).

- Aging volunteer firefighters (1998 to 2020): 50-59 year olds saw a huge 49% increase, and the number of volunteers 60+ years old more than doubled.

One doesn't need to be mathematician to see that this formula isn't balanced. Essentially, we have a quarter less people to do triple the amount of work. In any other business or industry this would be unsustainable. However, volunteer first responders have stepped up to the plate and answered the call. This however has not been done without consequence. Burnout is a real thing that can manifest in erosion of morale and implosion, causing serious issues for a department. While this phenomenon has developed, the amount of training required for first responders has increased exponentially, making it more difficult for the average person to join and onboard quickly. So, at a time when members are needed most, it has gotten slower for them to do so. While this training is necessary, it makes it difficult to adequately support an aging volunteer base quickly.

These are just some of the issues plaguing departments today. They are real issues, and often lack real solutions as the problems continue to fester. The main issue that I have personally seen is that fire/EMS departments lack access and knowledge of a framework and tools to use in order to accurately identify problems and develop solutions that last.

Quality improvement can help to create a comprehensive solution that addresses the true root cause of a problem and is conducted in a way that can generate results that meet a goal reliably and is sustainable. As mentioned above, in today's world departments don't have the luxury of misidentifying a problem, wasting effort on solutions that won't work or aren't sustainable, or managing staff in a way that leads to burnout . . . because everyday departments are having to close their doors or are having their budgets slashed. This is where the V.I.P.E.R. Improvement Model comes into play. This model uses tools and techniques that are bundled by business discipline, move from planning to solution, and embody certain values (Variance Inhibiting, Performance,

Efficiency, and Reliability) that permeate throughout the system. These tools and techniques are used extensively for quality improvement in many other industries to great effect. So, when your department needs to improve or fix something, think quality improvement. Think V.I.P.E.R.

Credentials and the Need for this Book

My background in the fire service includes over a decade of experience as a volunteer firefighter and EMT, with escalating responsibility as both an operational and administrative officer. As a profession I have worked in healthcare, specifically hospitals, for over ten years within quality improvement departments. My job has been to identify root causes to problems, create more efficient workflows, and above all improve both patient safety and satisfaction while reducing preventable harm. I further have several certifications that provide tools to help in this endeavor, including LEAN Six Sigma Black and Green Belts, CPHQ (Certified Professional in Healthcare Quality), and a Doctorate in Business Administration and Healthcare Management. I am also affiliated with several leadership organizations, including Leadership Southern Maryland and the Leadership Academy with Johns Hopkins Armstrong Institute for Patient Safety and Quality.

An interesting observation I have made is that I have seldom seen any of these tools and techniques used in my 10+ years volunteering at fire/EMS departments to the same extent that I have at hospitals. *Why is that?* These tools are used across many industries, starting in engineering, manufacturing, and supply chain operations almost 100 years ago. With issues as serious as those outlined above, it makes sense to use some serious tools. Hence the inspiration for writing this book. I want to make these tools available to my fellow first responders in a way that is easily understood using fire/EMS examples. Further, I have created a framework (V.I.P.E.R. Improvement Model) specifically for the fire/EMS industry as this industry is nuanced and requires several additions to typical improvement models. Most improvement models don't include elements of strategic planning, marketing, or human resources. However, fire/EMS departments need these elements to set priorities/goals, recruitment/retention, fundraising/community impact, and correctly motivating members. Therefore, these elements are included alongside typical improvement tools like process control charts, root cause analysis, risk management, and change management. Of note, a new tool was also developed for change management (B.U.R.N. Change Management Model) unique to the first responder industry. The V.I.P.E.R. model includes all these elements in a way that is interconnected and moves seamlessly.

How to Read and Use this Book

This text begins with an overview of the V.I.P.E.R. Improvement Model. The discussion will begin with how to use the model, what the values within the acronym mean, and its purpose. From there, each chapter is dedicated to a separate element of the model. The chapters progress in the general flow that an improvement project should take. First, strategic planning occurs with creating a mission, vision, values, S.M.A.R.T. goals, SWOT, and balanced scorecard. Next, the quality improvement channel can be taken which includes process control (normal variation, control charts, run charts) and then root cause analysis (5 Why's, pareto charts, fishbone charts). At the same time the internally facing channel can be used, which stresses strategic human resources management (superstars/steadies/nonplayers, motivation). Again at the same time, the externally facing channel can be used, which stresses marketing (5P's, 3C's, forecasting). These efforts then converge on a solution which is implemented using change management (B.U.R.N. Model). Lastly, the continuous improvement cycle is used to make sure the department is always moving forward to reduce risk through risk management (Failure Mode and Effects Analysis (FMEA), SAFER Matrix), which would then cycle back to the change management section again.

Chapter 2: V.I.P.E.R. Improvement Model

While the tools outlined in this book can be utilized individually, they can become exponentially more effective if used within a system. The system created for improvement within the fire and EMS service is the V.I.P.E.R. (Variance Inhibiting, Performance, Efficiency, and Reliability) Improvement Model. The V.I.P.E.R. model leverages each management discipline and underlying tools in a way that is synergistic (see Figure 1).

Figure 1. V.I.P.E.R. Improvement Model

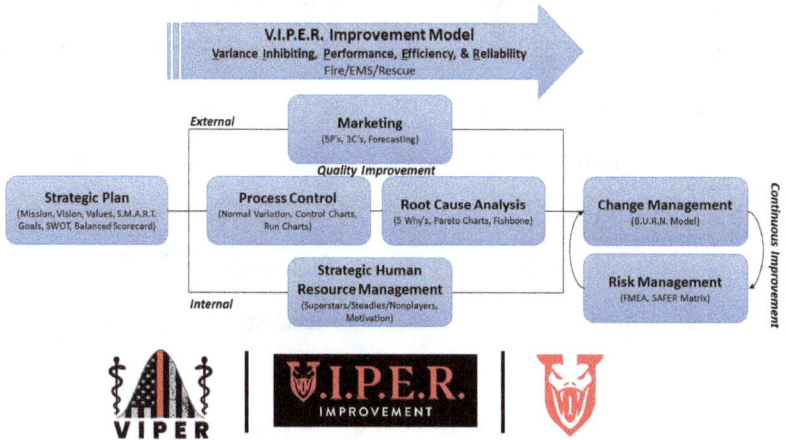

V.I.P.E.R. Improvement Model Flow

Each of the V.I.P.E.R. acronym terms are values represented by the model. Each of these terms permeate throughout the model and should be thought of as a guide and motivation when using the tools outlined. Specifically made for the fire and EMS service, the V.I.P.E.R. model provides strategic planning, process control, root cause analysis, the ability to market within a volunteer atmosphere, managing human resources in a thoughtful way, how to hardwire change, and how to think proactively and manage risk. The strategy is to begin by using a department's strategic plan as a launching point to set priorities and an overall route to follow for the next several years. At this point the model flow separates into three separate channels that can be done concurrently: quality improvement, external, and internal. The quality improvement channel starts by measuring the elements of a strategic plan using process control charts, which can be further evaluated for unstable conditions using a root cause analysis. At the same time, a marketing strategy can be employed to communicate with a department's community, stakeholders, and patients and can assist in recruitment in the externally facing channel. Concurrently a strategic human resources management strategy can be used to promote retention through optimization of human capital by understanding motivational development in the internal channel. These three channels all converge, or funnel, into change management, which is the step where the improvements identified in the three channels are then implemented and hardwired. Once the department is on stable ground after these steps have been completed, it can test and probe for any further potential weaknesses or risks using risk management techniques, which will then cycle back to change management as the solutions identified to mitigate risks are then implemented and hardwired (this cycle is known as continuous improvement). This is the general flow of the V.I.P.E.R. Improvement Model.

V.I.P.E.R. - Variance Inhibiting

Variance Inhibiting refers to limiting process variance or deviation, and therefore reducing risk. Having variance in a process creates instability, and instability equals risk, patient harm, or unintended consequences. A process should be reliable and inhibit, or prevent, variance. The model expresses this through the measuring of process variance using control charts, mitigating negative variance through root cause analysis, and preventing it though risk management practices such as Failure Mode and Effects Analysis (FMEA). Variance Inhibiting and risk mitigation can also be accomplished through forecasting within marketing, which prepares a department regarding proactive resource allocation.

V.I.P.E.R. - Performance

Performance can be defined as the method of achieving an objective and the degree to which a device/person conducts an action successfully. Performance therefore refers to accomplishing a goal and acts as a measurement of effectiveness. This concept is instilled in the model as the S.M.A.R.T. (Specific, Measurable,

Attainable, Reasonable, Time-Based) goals derived from the mission, vision, and values in a strategic plan guide actions and tactics for their accomplishment. Further, the performance element is embedded in the measurement of a process that relates directly to control charts. Using the correct motivation found in strategic human resource management can improve the performance and output of department members. Lastly, communicating a department's performance to the community or external stakeholders is accomplished through marketing.

V.I.P.E.R. - *Efficiency*

Efficiency is operating in a manner that utilizes the least amount of resources to accomplish a goal and to reduce waste. This concept is prevalent throughout the model, as fire/EMS departments use techniques to maximize their efforts despite constrained budgets, decreasing volunteer personnel, and limited time. Uncovering inefficiency is the purpose of root cause analysis and control charts, while maximizing efficiency of personnel through correct motivation is found within strategic human resource management.

V.I.P.E.R. - *Reliability*

Reliability speaks to consistency, dependability, stability, and accuracy. Process stability is synergistic with reliability, which is measured using control charts, while implementing a new process or solution using change management creates a new reliable process. Risk management techniques such as FMEA (Failure Mode Effects Analysis) and the SAFER Matrix increase reliability by reducing risk.

Inspiration for V.I.P.E.R.

The V.I.P.E.R. model was also developed specifically as an improvement model for fire and EMS departments because of the analogy that an actual viper conveys. The viper is an ambush predator that conserves its energy in camouflage until it's ready to strike. Then it unleashes all its power to attack, or defend itself. In a similar way, fire and EMS departments are the viper. They wait at the station until the tones drop. When they do, crews launch into action just like a striking viper, with precision and accuracy, unleashing all the experience, training, knowledge, and skills acquired to get a knock on the fire, extricate the victim, deescalate the hazmat situation, or provide emergency services to a patient. The snake analogy is further justified as it is prevalent throughout our EMS community in other ways. As another example, the Star of Life found on many EMS insignias include the Rod of Asclepius, which is a staff wrapped in a snake that represents healing. The viper therefore serves as a great inspiration and icon for the improvement model within the fire/EMS service.

Purpose for V.I.P.E.R.

The purpose for the V.I.P.E.R. Improvement Model is to fill the gap experienced by many departments who are left to figure out on their own how to lead and improve a department. This can be especially difficult if one doesn't have a background in leadership, management, or quality improvement. Further, many resources currently available for these topics are not tailored specifically for the fire and EMS service. They are tailored instead for other industries such as hospitals, manufacturing, or transportation. This makes it difficult to translate and utilize this information as it lacks examples and nuances specific to fire/EMS. The V.I.P.E.R. Improvement Model is developed specifically for the purpose of providing tools to improve within a framework that allows for them to work synergistically within fire and EMS departments.

Chapter 3: Strategic Planning - The Pre-Plan for Your Department

Do you find that your department is always reacting, or even sometimes over-reacting, to the latest crisis or trend? Does this cause your department to rehash the same issues over and over again? You're not alone; it can be difficult to look beyond the next call. In order to take a more proactive stance in your department, a strategic plan can help. Essentially, it's conducting a pre-plan for your department. Similar to a pre-plan, it identifies what your organization is, what the hazards are, what resources are available, and how best to mitigate risk while executing your objective.

A strategic plan is an effective way for a fire or EMS department to determine where it wants to go, how it wants to grow, and the path it needs to take to get there. The planning process itself is a healthy activity that can help illuminate what the department does well, how it can improve, and what it values. A strategic plan can also help insulate the department from risks associated with investing time and resources on activities that may not fit with the department's goals. Having a strategic plan provides a roadmap to success.

Ideally a strategic plan should be updated and reassessed every 3-5 years. The members to include in its development should comprise key stakeholders, including both administrative and operational leadership, Board of Directors, key senior members, or bright and rising members. Having diverse representation prevents the phenomenon known as *group think*, which occurs when a collection of like-minded individuals proposes single-minded solutions that lack alternative perspectives. Ensuring a diverse group will yield the best and most innovative solutions.

Mission, Vision, Values

A strategic plan has several elements that are developed in sequence. These include developing a mission and vision, values and goals, and monitoring. The mission of the department encompasses its purpose for existence. Why is it here? What does it do? A vision is a forward-looking statement that articulates what the department wants to be. The vision statement needs to be transformative, or even *disruptive*. The vision statement is by definition a challenge to the status quo or the current state, because as a department the goal is to improve in some aspect. "To become the most reliable department in our county" can be used as an example. The department needs to come to terms with the fact that in some aspects there might be room for improvement to become more reliable. In order to accomplish this vision, goals could be set around reliability: improving scratch rates, helping neighboring departments with fill-ins, increasing representation and attendance at county and regional meetings, increase member proficiency with more frequent training. This vision sets the tone for where the department will prioritize efforts over the coming years.

These two statements are the launching position with which the department will use to develop the rest of the plan. The mission and vision will also act as the department's source of truth, in that when decisions are to be made, they should be evaluated against if it fits within the mission and vision.

After the mission and vision are identified, a department should deliberate which values are most consistent with its nature. Values are altruistic words or short phrases that display what the department stands for and what it holds as an expectation for members or staff to exemplify. A department should seek to identify 3-5 values it wishes to embody and represent.

SWOT Analysis

Next are the development of goals to reach the department's vision. A tool to help uncover this is a SWOT analysis. SWOT stands for the department's Strengths, Weaknesses, Opportunities, and Threats. This is commonly displayed as a 2x2 matrix grid (Figure 2), with strengths in the upper left quadrant, weaknesses in the upper right quadrant, opportunities in the lower left quadrant, and threats in the lower right quadrant. Once the grid is populated with the SWOT elements, they can be addressed and operationalized through goal development.

Figure 2. SWOT Analysis

SWOT	Positive	Negative
Internal	Strengths	Weaknesses
External	Opportunities	Threats

Strengths and weaknesses pertain to the internal environment, or the department itself. What are the things the department does well? What does it excel at? What are things that the department needs to improve? Where does the department fall short or struggle? Strength examples could include such items as the department has a strong lifetime member base or conducts robust training in-house. Weaknesses could include items such as low new member intake numbers, or aging apparatus.

The opportunities and threats pertain to the external environment. Opportunities are things that could positively impact the department, and threats are things that could have a negative impact. These could include such elements as the impact of socio-political forces, economy, climate, laws/regulations, or population health patterns. Practical examples of threats could include hurricane season for departments located along the Atlantic Coast or snowstorms in the Midwest, Covid or similar outbreaks, the opioid epidemic, or inflation and its impact on prices for fire-gear and medical supplies. Opportunities may include such things as new firefighting tactics, new technologies, new grants, or new partnerships with neighboring departments or agencies.

Once the SWOT analysis is conducted, the department will develop goals that leverage a department's strengths to overcome a weakness or develop an opportunity. These opportunities would be crafted in development of new strengths to curtail a weakness or prevent a threat. Threats should be acknowledged and prepared for in order to insulate the department from risk.

S.M.A.R.T. Goals

Goal-setting is an essential element of any successful fire department. The process of goal-setting tells a story: where you were, where you are, and where you want to be. Essentially, without goal-setting it is impossible for a department to understand if they have been successful or not. Further, goal-setting can help to improve the engagement of your officers and promote their professional growth.

Effective goals are S.M.A.R.T. (Specific, Measurable, Attainable, Reasonable, Time-Based). S.M.A.R.T. goal-setting is a tool that can be utilized to ensure a comprehensive goal is set. Goals should be specific, in that they should not be broad. They should include exactly what is to be accomplished and who is responsible. The goal should also be measurable, or quantifiable and tied to a metric or number. The goal should be attainable, in that it should be realistic and able to be met. The goal should be reasonable, where it is within the department's capability to impact and not something that is beyond their influence. The goal should also be time-based with a deadline. Milestone dates can also be included to ensure progress is being made.

Let's give an example of a S.M.A.R.T. goal, with the focus on the reduction of workplace injuries at a firehouse. In this example, the department has updated its strategic plan and has identified a weakness of increased workplace injuries at the firehouse, particularly in lower back and lower extremity injuries. Also, the department has committed to a strategic value of working in a safe environment as it has become concerned with injuries and the increase of cancer rates among firefighters. A S.M.A.R.T. goal might include the following: *Reduce the number of lower back and lower extremity workplace injuries from an average of 2.5 per month to 1 per month within the next 90 days through the use of a flexibility program developed in coordination with a local physical therapy practice.* This goal is specific in that it highlights the exact type of injuries of lower back and lower extremities and identifies the exact process improvement of a flexibility program developed by physical therapy experts. The goal is measurable as it points to a baseline period of 2.5 injuries per month with the goal of reducing it to 1 injury per month. The goal is attainable as it is approximately 1.5 less injuries per month but is not reduced to the unattainable number of 0 per month. The goal is reasonable as it aligns with the value of working in a safe environment. It is further reasonably within the scope of the firehouse to affect. The goal is also time-based as it states the average of 1 injury per month will be reached within 90 days.

Goal-setting can also help at the individual level, particularly with officer accountability, transparency, and professional growth. An officer may be placed in charge of overseeing a program, such as pre-planning, apparatus check-offs, or improving the turnover process. Simply telling the officer they are in charge of overseeing this program or telling them to simply improve it and just "get it done" is a recipe for not meeting expectations because an expectation has not been set. To set an expectation that the officer can be held accountable to, goal-setting is needed.

As an example, let's set a S.M.A.R.T. goal for an officer placed in charge of ensuring members are completing their apparatus check-offs. *Ensure each of the 6 apparatus is checked off at the beginning of each shift (within first 30 minutes) with greater than 90% compliance.* This goal is specific in that it references the number of apparatus included in the check-off program, when during the shift they are to occur, and the time duration they should be started. The goal is measurable as it includes the number of apparatus, the amount of time allowable to begin the check-off each shift, and the targeted percent compliance. The goal is attainable as it allows for a 10% buffer to account for unforeseen circumstances such as that piece of apparatus being committed on a call during the change of shift. The goal is reasonable as this is a common expectation to ensure apparatus operational readiness, and within the officer's capability to impact through various oversight mechanisms such as setting up an inbox for completed check-offs to ensure they are being done. In this example, the time-based element is utilized through the 30-minute timeframe the check-off is to be completed within at the beginning of a shift. This goal provides the officer with a frame of reference with which to benchmark their success. They now know exactly what they need to do to be successful in meeting expectations. Further, the officer can now highlight this success in a meaningful way during any performance review as a way they have followed directions, accomplished their directive, and made a positive impact on the department.

Goal-setting can help a fire department focus on critical activities as opposed to wasteful endeavors, as goal-setting focuses efforts towards meeting specific expectations. This focus can assist the department in keeping a forward-thinking mentality as the goal sets the bar that must be met. This mentality prevents rehashing of previous issues, or inefficient rework, as goal-setting adds both clarity and collaborative efforts working in the same direction.

Lastly, utilization of goal-setting can be used at both the departmental level (financial goals, operational goals, or recruitment/retention goals) and at an individual level (roles and responsibilities, professional growth, or learning and development).

Balanced Scorecard

From here the strategic plan is monitored to ensure progress is being made in the right direction. A Balanced Scorecard can help, where Key Performance Indicators (KPI's) are routinely monitored. This tool provides a comprehensive measurement of a department's performance, and usually includes 1-3 measures per section. The sections on a Balanced Scorecard include metrics specific to finance, customer, quality/process, and people. The finance section includes financial health metrics such as costs, savings, or fundraising amounts. The customer section includes the perspective from those which the department serves. This is typically the community or patients but could also include other stakeholders the department works with such as hospitals, neighboring departments, or local health departments. Metrics might include any survey data or community event attendance. The quality/process section measures performance improvement. This could include such metrics as scratch rates, response times, or personnel per call. The people section includes the human resource perspective. This could include metrics such as number of new members, retention rates, staff injuries, or internal staff satisfaction survey results. Each metric should aim to *monitor* the progress of meeting a *goal* that is consistent with a *value* that achieves the *mission* of the department and helps it move towards realizing its *vision*.

Chapter Summary

A strategic plan can help a fire or EMS department focus on critical activities as opposed to wasteful endeavors and can assist in decision-making since decisions are assessed in their alignment to the elements of the strategic plan. In this way the department is prepared and forward-thinking, similar to a pre-plan, where risks are prepared for in advance and a framework already exists to lead the department towards positive outcomes that aren't wasteful. This is the beginning of the V.I.P.E.R. Improvement Model from which all other activities branch out from.

Chapter 4: Process Control – Managing for Stability

After the strategic plan is completed, the next step in the V.I.P.E.R. model is to enter either the internal, external, or quality improvement channel. The quality improvement channel is comprised of two sections, Process Control and Root Cause Analysis. This chapter is dedicated to the Process Control section.

Normal Distribution, Bell Curves, and Management

One does not need to be a statistician to leverage the benefits of understanding a bell curve. Having a basic understanding of the concept can yield great insight into the management of a fire/EMS department. A bell curve is a physical depiction of a set of data or circumstances, with a peak in the middle and tapering tails on either side. It is divided in half by a center line and boxed in near the ends of each side. The center line is the average. The line near the left tail is the Lower Control Limit (LCL), and the line near the right end is the Upper Control Limit (UCL). This is the basic representation of what's called normal distribution, which constitutes the majority of data. This normal distribution stacks up in this manner because of standard deviation, which is a statistical metric that measures the amount of variation or dispersion from the average. A lower standard deviation means the data is high clustered around the average, a high standard deviation means the data points are more spread out. We discuss this because a normal distribution has distinct standard deviation (sometimes referred to as Sigma) levels. See Figure 3 for more details. One standard deviation above and below the average includes 68.2% of the data, two standard deviations above and below the average includes 95.4% of the data, and three standard deviations above and below the average includes 99.7% of the data (this is where the UCL and LCL are set). This is important because it sets the foundation for applying management concepts. Essentially, it would be very statistically unlikely for data to fall outside these third sigma levels. We call these rare cases outliers or special cause variation (as a special condition is occurring outside of the normal circumstances that is creating a value abnormally high or low). This will become quite important when interpreting control charts.

Figure 3. Normal Distribution Bell Curve

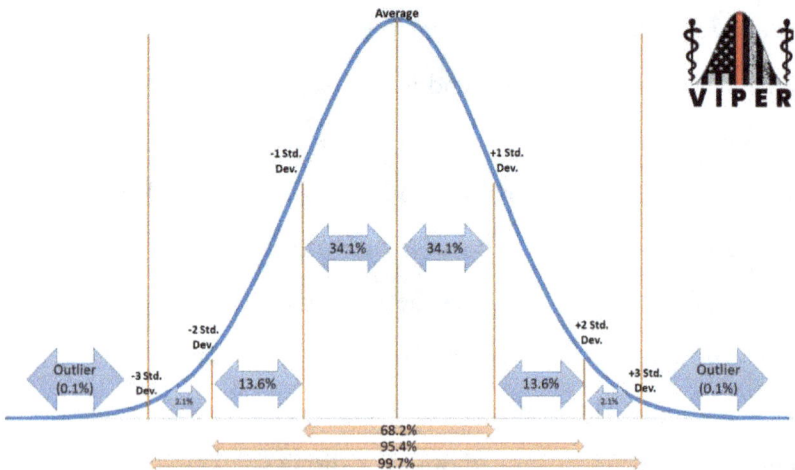

Using rough estimates and the above information, one can surmise that a healthy majority of the data (within one standard deviation is 68.2%; or approximately 2/3) should cluster around average conditions. This is where the management comes in. Knowing this concept, a leader within the department knows that the majority of the time (2/3) things are going to occur as they normally would (i.e. close to the average). In some rare cases, things will occur well (1/6) or poorly (1/6). In looking forward at the Human Resources chapter, this is the exact distribution for the three staff categories. The majority of staff are steadies (60%-70%), with a small proportion on the top end as superstars (10%-20%), and another small proportion at the bottom end as nonplayers (10%-15%). The percentages match up with the bell curve above exactly (2/3, 1/6, and 1/6), this is no coincidence, this is normal distribution at work in the real world. The majority of house fires are put out without bad outcomes, while a small number may result in crew injury and some may result in a victim rescue. The majority of the time apparatus will operate without a problem, while a small proportion of the time there are breakdowns. The majority of the time departments will meet their budget, while a smaller amount of the time there will be a deficit, and others a surplus.

Bittel (1972) speaks to this phenomenon in his text *The Nine Master Keys to Management*. Specifically, understanding this normal distribution in the real world gives a manager a balanced outlook as opposed to being a prisoner of the moment during extreme events. Bittel (1972) discusses that this understanding and balanced outlook means managers will aim for rewarding goals but are not derailed by minor setbacks, that they expect solid performance from their crews but do not expect perfection, that apparatus and equipment will typically work fine but on occasion may break down, "in short the professional manager has a balanced view of his resources, his goals, and his chances for their attainment. And he bases this on his knowledge of the principles of normal distribution and statistical probability" (p. 52). Essentially, there is a small chance that the best or worst outcome might happen, but there is a high probability that something more mundane will most likely occur. Just as the nonplayer (low performing staff) will point out all the issues and failures and make it sound like this is the majority, astute managers and officers will know that this is not the case due to normal distribution.

As a quick aside, the reader of this book may ask why such an old reference (1972) for a management concept? Surely there is a more modern book or article to cite? The reader would be correct, there are plenty of publications that could be referenced in the 50 years since this book was published. The reasoning is two-fold. First, this is a fantastic book and one of the best resources on practical management with concepts that are still pertinent today. Second, it reinforces the fundamental problem cited at the beginning of this book…why on earth haven't the concepts of normal distribution and control charts made their way into the fire and EMS industry over the last 50 years at the same saturation levels as other industries such as manufacturing, transportation, and healthcare? I bought this book in an antique store…please let that statement sink in a second. We as an industry deserve to have these tools made available, and understood, so that they can be leveraged to improve our industry. This information has been available for decades, and it's about time fire/EMS utilize them as well.

Control Charts

When reviewing a process, it can be very beneficial to see the data in graphical format, and using a line chart is typically what people use. This graphical representation views your data over time. This could be calls, fundraising amounts, scratch rates etc. The shortcoming of using a line chart is it can have subjective interpretation. Does it look like it is trending up? Is this one data point that drops significant? It looks like its bouncing back and forth, but we aren't sure quite what to make of it? If one is going to use a graph to depict data, it needs to be meaningful, tell a story, and have analytic value.

Graphs that are meaningful connect to a purpose and satisfy a need. For instance, a department can't interpret the magnitude of its cost variances from a data table, and so need a graph to illustrate. *Graphs that tell a story need to be grounded in context.* For example, a graph with several high points for scratch rates are annotated with the fact that the majority of the top runners all caught the flu at the same time. *Graphs that are analytical leverage statistics to provide insight.* This might include reviewing the mean (average) and the median (middle) of a line graph for fundraising amounts and finding that the average is significantly higher than the median. This could mean that there were several very large donations that would constitute as outliers, and after discovering this warrants a personal follow-up letter to these donors expressing gratitude (this phenomenon between a mean and median is significant, because a mean will take the average of all values in a dataset including any outliers, while a median will choose the middle value and thus insulates this value from outliers; so one might want to occasionally calculate both to see if any abnormally large/small values are "pulling" your mean away from a true center of the data, which might be more accurately represented with the median).

One type of chart that checks off all the requirements of being meaningful, tells a story, and has analytic value is the control chart. Control charts are the Cadillac of graphs, with the main goal of determining if a process is in control or out of control. These control charts have been used for many decades in manufacturing, engineering, transportation, and healthcare as a means to understand, interpret, and control processes. As proof of its maturity, Duncan (1974) a Johns Hopkins University professor of statistics and mathematics articulates in his text *Quality Control and Industrial Statistics*, "a control chart is a device for describing in concrete terms what a state of statistical control is; second, a device for attaining control; and, third, a device for judging whether control has been attained" (p. 376). And yes, I found this book in an antique shop as well (the fourth edition, the first edition was published in 1952). This book is a tried-and-true resource for quality control. This again reflects just how long these charts have been used in other industries and are therefore overdue for application within the fire/EMS industry.

These charts have the analytic value that utilizes standard deviation, tell a story through specific statistical rules that will articulate if a statistical shift is occurring or not, and is meaningful because it assesses if a process is stable or unstable. Duncan (1974) indicates that control charts relate to management in that they serve to define the goal one seeks to achieve, that they can be used as a tool to attain this goal, and that they can be used to determine if the goal has actually been reached. The author notes that control charts

31

differentiate a process between chance variation (or typical/random variation that would normally occur within a process) and special cause variation (or outliers, shifts, trends). Essentially, if a review of a process using a control chart finds the data to fall within the standard deviation lines in a typical pattern, then this is chance variation and there are no special assignable causes to investigate. A control chart is essentially the trending representation of a bell curve with normal distribution. A control chart looks like a line chart, but also has a center line (mean), a UCL (Upper Control Limit), and a LCL (Lower Control Limit) just like a bell curve. To understand this connection, see Figure 4 which turns a bell curve on its side next to a control chart.

Figure 4. Bell Curve and Control Chart Connection

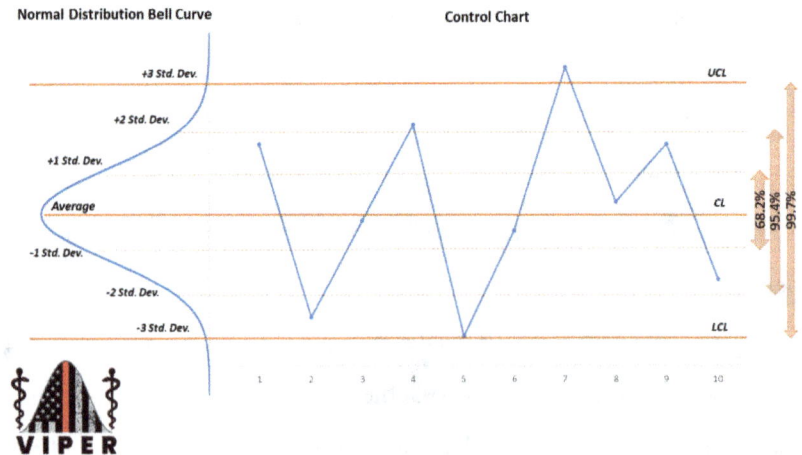

Do you see how the center line (CL), UCL/LCL, and the other standard deviation lines match up? The normal distribution percentages also apply in the exact same manner. This means that the majority of one's data should cluster around the mean with the same distribution percentages (68.2% between +1 and -1 std. dev., 95.4% between +2 and -2 std. dev., and 99.7% between +3 and -3 std. dev. (aka UCL and LCL)). This distribution brings stability and reliability into the conversation. A process should be stable, in that it should be *reliable*. Incidents *rely* on a water supply being established. Incidents *rely* on the hydraulic tools operating correctly. Incidents *rely* on the truck company forcing the door, throwing ladders, and securing utilities. When things become unreliable, they become unstable, and this unstableness is based on variance. Variance means things are not occurring as they should. And from a statistical perspective, standard deviation is actually calculated by taking the square root of a dataset's variance. This shows the link between variance and standard deviation lines. Therefore, using normal distribution within a control chart can measure process variance by viewing if data points are falling outside the standard deviation lines to determine if a process is stable and reliable. A deviation/variance would indicate an unstable condition, which would warrant an investigation into why these data points are deviating. This could be a negative, in which case one of the root cause tools (see Ch. 4) would need to be used to uncover the source of the instability. This could also be positive, in that the department has instituted an improvement or solution, and thus would want to see a deviation from the status quo which was previously not meeting expectations. Therefore, when using a control chart and special cause variation is occurring on the favorable side of the central line, then it should be investigated to replicate. If special cause variation is occurring on the unfavorable side, then it should be investigated to eliminate. This links to the Variance Inhibiting value that defines V.I.P.E.R.

To create a control chart, it is easiest to use a software program specifically made to do so. There are many different types, which one can find online with a simple search. Most are standalone applications, while others may work as an extension within a program like MS Excel. A department should choose a program that that fits best with respect to ease of use, cost, and support. Some examples of software programs include QI Macros, Minitab, or SPSS.

Control Chart Rules

Once a department chooses a control chart software program, it can begin to track various metrics to evaluate process stability. A great place to start are the KPI's used to populate the balanced scorecard within the strategic plan. As a standing example going forward, let's use a department's scratch rate. In order to evaluate a control chart, there are several rules that may trigger. If they do, then this means an unstable condition is occurring. This can be good or bad depending on which side of the CL it is occurring. For the scratch rate example, lower is better, so you would want to investigate if a rule occurs on the favorable side and replicate; or eliminate if it was on the unfavorable higher side. A set of some pertinent statistical rules are cited below in Figure 5. There are several other rules, however for the purposes of the fire/EMS service, these should be adequate to determine if a shift, trend, outlier, or any over-control conditions are occurring.

Figure 5: Control Chart Rules

Rule Number	Description	Impact
1	1 data point above UCL or below LCL	Outlier
2	2/3 data points outside 2 std. dev.	Shift
3	4/5 data points outside 1 std. dev.	Shift
4	9 data points in a row above/below CL	Shift
5	6 data points in a row increasing/decreasing	Trend
6	15 data points in a row within +/-1 std. dev. of CL	Over-Control

The reason these rules exist is linked to predictability of the normal distribution. Essentially, it is incredibly rare for any of these to occur randomly. In fact, when the numbers are run each rule has less than a 1% chance of randomly occurring. This gives considerable credibility for when they do occur, as there is something going on that is having a statistically significant influence on the process. Let's look at what these rules would look like on a control chart (Figure 6) using the scratch rate example.

Figure 6. Scratch Rate Control Chart – Rule Examples

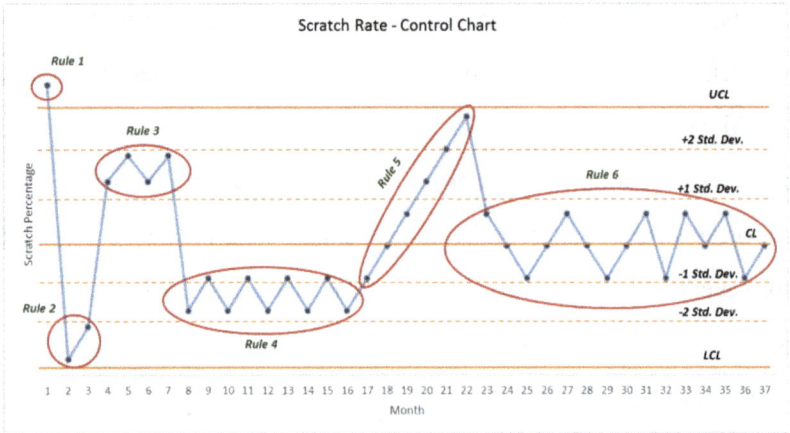

When interpreting a control chart and any of these rule conditions occur, a discussion with other subject matter experts should occur using a root cause analysis to identify what is causing the impact. These rules add objective criteria for interpretation, instead of guesses as to if something looks like it is improving or not on a regular line chart. If a department has implemented a solution, they would want to find one of these rules occurring on the favorable side of the central line, and as this becomes the new norm using change management tools, this change in process would be the new start to the control chart and the standard deviations would need to be recalculated based on this fresh start. As one can see, a control chart needs quite a few data points for the rules to activate, with a rule of thumb of at least 20 being ideal. If more data points are needed, consider segmenting the data by time. Instead of annual data points, try quarterly or monthly data to give additional data points. One can also try bi-weekly, weekly, or daily as well. Keep in mind that enough data is needed to evaluate for each data point, so use judgment when considering timeframes. One doesn't want to cut their data too slim and not have any data to evaluate.

Types of Control Charts

There are various types of control charts to use based on the data one is trying to analyze. While some software programs will evaluate one's data and choose the most appropriate chart, others will not. Therefore, below is a brief overview of the most typical types of control charts one might need if one is required to choose themselves:

- Variable Data – Anything that is measured and often contains a decimal (weight, money, time, length etc.)
  - Use an Individual X Chart.
- Attribute Data – Counted data, which is usually a whole number (number of errors, items, injuries, people etc.)
  - Use a C chart.
  - If you have a percentage, the numerator and denominator can be used to create a P chart. This

will cause the control limits to fluctuate based on the size of the denominator.

There are additional control chart types, however based on the data fire/EMS departments are most likely to encounter, the above charts are the most likely to be used.

Run Charts

Having trouble with control charts, or don't have the resources to create them? Don't worry, there is another option that can help. Known as run charts, these charts can also be used to interpret department data.

Run charts are less complicated to make than control charts, but still offer more analytical power than simple line charts. Run charts however lack the ability of control charts to understand how stable a process is, yet can still help identify signals in a department's data. The other benefit is that a department doesn't need special software to create a run chart like a control chart; a simple program like MS Excel is sufficient.

To build a run chart, start with a simple line chart of your data. Next, calculate the median. Add the median line to the center of your chart. That's it, you're done. You don't need to calculate sigma levels or control limits like control charts.

Run charts have four rules for interpretation that act as signals. Rule one is a *shift*, which has at least six data points on one side of the median line (skip values that fall on the median line). This is a signal based on statistical probability that something nonrandom is occurring, because for this to occur randomly would be a chance of 3 in 1000.

Rule two is a *trend*, which is defined as 5 or more data points in a row going up or down (if a data point repeats itself consecutively, count the first instance and ignore any further that might repeat). This is also a signal of special cause variation, and that something significant is occurring.

Rule three is a *run*, which is any time a line between data points crosses the median center line. To count the total number of runs, count the number of times a line crosses the median then add one. A run chart can actually have too few or too many runs based on how many total data points are present. To figure this out a table exists which tells the exact number of runs that constitute too few or too many; simply perform an internet search for "run chart table." For example, if a chart has twelve data points for each month in a year, too few runs is three or less, and too many would be eleven or more. As another example, if you have 30 data points for each day in a month, too few runs would be eleven or less, and too many would be 21 or more. Just look up the table to see what the limits are for too few or too many runs the line graph is crossing the median line. Too many runs indicate two possible distributions of data. An example of this rule is there might be two different performance levels for two different work shifts (night/day), or one level of work on weekdays and another on weekends. Too few runs can indicate a shift is coming in the data.

Rule four is an *astronomical point*, which is a data point that is obviously different from the rest of the data (similar to an outlier in control charts outside the control limits). This rule is unique because it is subjective and based on judgement, the other three are based on probability like control chart rules.

In summary, if a department doesn't have the resources to support control charts, run charts are the next best thing. Run charts allow a department to view signals in the data that something significant is occurring that is not random and should be investigated. If the rule is occurring on the unfavorable side of the median line, identify the root cause and stop it. If it is occurring on the favorable side of the median, determine ways to support it. Finally, if the department has implemented an improvement and is looking for a positive impact, look for one of these rules to occur to show that it has taken hold.

Chapter Summary

The understanding of how normal distribution works is an effective way to gain understanding of management principles within the fire and EMS service. Further, control charts operationalize this concept into a tool that can be practically utilized to investigate unstable conditions occurring within a department. This process can reduce the amount of variation in a process to make it more stable, improve the performance of a department as it is more effectively measured, focus attention on unstable conditions that may reduce the efficiency of resources or be causing waste, and create a more reliable process as special causes are investigated and eliminated. Run charts are another option to analyze data for signals of significance if control charts are too burdensome. Process control highlights identifying and reducing variation relating to the Variance Inhibiting value, measures the performance of a metric and process highlighting the Performance value, can identify inefficiencies which exemplifies the Efficiency value, and seeks the ultimate goal of improving stability embodying the Reliability value.

Dr. David Hupp

Chapter 5: Root Cause Analysis

At some point your department will experience a problem where the cause isn't immediately identifiable. Inevitably everyone involved will have their own opinion, based on their own knowledge and experience, as to what the "real" problem is. These differing and sometimes strong opinions can lead to conflict and finger-pointing, without any real process improvement occurring. A technique to systematically and objectively untangle and identify the source of a problem is known as quality improvement through root cause analysis.

Within the V.I.P.E.R. Improvement Model, this step is found in the quality improvement channel after process control charts. Ideally what will happen is that control charts will be developed based on factors identified in the strategic plan. Once the control charts are created, they are monitored to identify if any unstable conditions are occurring via the statistical rules. If one of the rules are activated, then a root cause analysis would need to be done to identify why this subpar performance is occurring (because the control chart has established that it isn't random, and that something statistically significant is occurring and needs to be investigated).

Defining Root Cause Analysis

The central idea of a root cause analysis is that focus should be given to solving causes as opposed to symptoms. The analogy stems (pardon the pun) from pulling weeds, where if you only focus on the symptoms of a problem (ripping off leaves) and not on the critical driver of the problem (roots), then the weed will grow back. This phenomenon can manifest itself when dealing with personnel as the source of a problem. The focus should be placed on fixing processes as opposed to solely focusing on the person. Yes, if someone was acting maliciously and is obviously culpable it is imperative to fix the personnel issue. But frequently the failure in a process is a breakdown that caused the person to fail. Typically, when a failure occurs the person responsible is reprimanded or even fired without further investigation, and then everyone moves on. However, if a person is fired, and the process that allowed the person to cause a failure isn't fixed, the next person to fill that role will have the same problem because the root cause was never truly fixed. For example, a member riding the right front seat for the first time failed to conduct a 360. It's important to find out why they failed to conduct it. Possibly in drilling down it is found out that during their onboarding the 360 isn't stressed with only minimal time dedicated to what it is, and practice isn't completed on how these are to be done on various types of incidents. By reprimanding the member and not fixing the process, people are still being trained inadequately in conducting a 360, and this problem can happen again.

There are three tools that can help to identify a root cause. These include 5 Why's, Pareto Charts, and the Fishbone Diagram. These tools can be used individually or in conjunction with one another. Ideally a group will be convened to discuss and populate the elements of these tools. This will ensure a diversity of perspectives is present, which will uncover blind spots and expose any critical drivers to the issue at hand. One person's perspective is typically not sufficient to adequately identify all the elements of a problem. It is imperative that members of this group feel empowered to speak in order to facilitate an open discussion.

5 Why's

The 5 Why's is an easy tool to use to get to the root of the problem. To use the tool, you simply ask "Why?" five times. You start with the actual problem and ask "why did this happen?" After the answer is given, ask again, "well, why did that happen?" Then continue until you have asked five times, and chances are you have arrived at the root cause to your issue, and focus should be dedicated to fixing this root cause. In fixing this cause, it will then automatically fix the other four symptoms identified during the drilldown. As an example, Figure 7 investigates the issue of a growing average age at a volunteer fire department.

Figure 7. 5 Why's Example

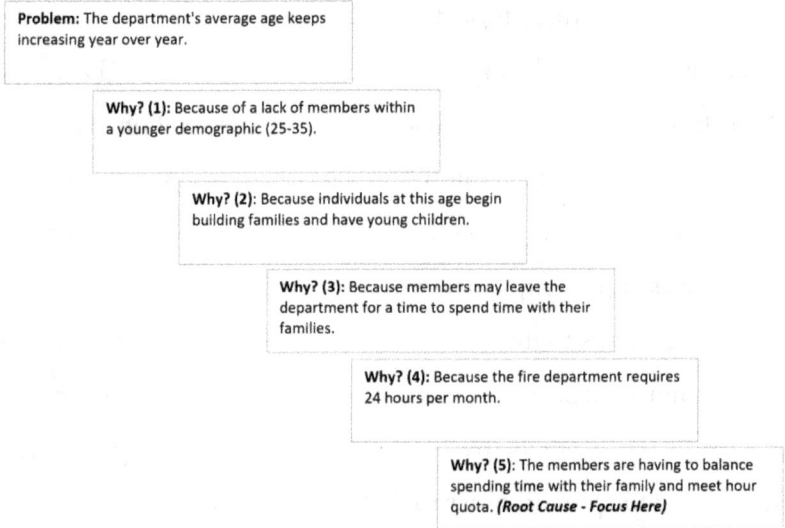

Problem: The department's average age keeps increasing year over year.

Why? (1): Because of a lack of members within a younger demographic (25-35).

Why? (2): Because individuals at this age begin building families and have young children.

Why? (3): Because members may leave the department for a time to spend time with their families.

Why? (4): Because the fire department requires 24 hours per month.

Why? (5): The members are having to balance spending time with their family and meet hour quota. *(Root Cause - Focus Here)*

As one can see, it isn't initially apparent that the issue causing a rising average age is family-balance. Hence the need to drill down. After the fifth why is asked, a potential solution could involve adding family dinners at the department to help alleviate the balance that is having to be maintained by the member between family responsibilities and volunteering. In this way when the member is staffing the station for their 24-hour quota they can still spend time with their family during the scheduled family dinner times.

Pareto Charts

Another tool that can be used to identify root causes is the pareto chart. This chart is based on the pareto principle. The pareto principle is a power law that has universal applicability. The pareto principle states that 80% of problems are derived from 20% of causes. This 20% is known as the vital few, which are the drivers for 80% of the output or problems. 80% of calls are run by 20% of the members (top runners). 80% of calls are located at 20% of addresses (frequent fliers). 80% of vehicle extrication calls occur at 20% of specific intersections (dangerous intersections). These are just several of the intuitive examples of how the pareto principle works. The visual depiction of the pareto principle is the pareto chart. A pareto chart is a bar graph that is sorted from largest to smallest, with a secondary line that shows the cumulative percentage of the bars. The idea is to focus on the bars (causes) that make up the top 20%. To create the chart, simply sort your data from largest to smallest and use a program like MS Excel to create a bar chart. Next, add a second column of data that calculates the cumulative percentage (the first datapoint is the top cause at X% of the total, the second data point is cumulative percentage of the top two bars, etc.) Add this as a line to the same graph. See Figure 8 for an example pareto chart investigating the number of housefires by neighborhood. Perhaps the department wants to review trending of where housefires are occurring, which could be used as the basis to focus outreach and prevention activities like National Night Out or smoke detector allotments.

Figure 8. Sample Pareto

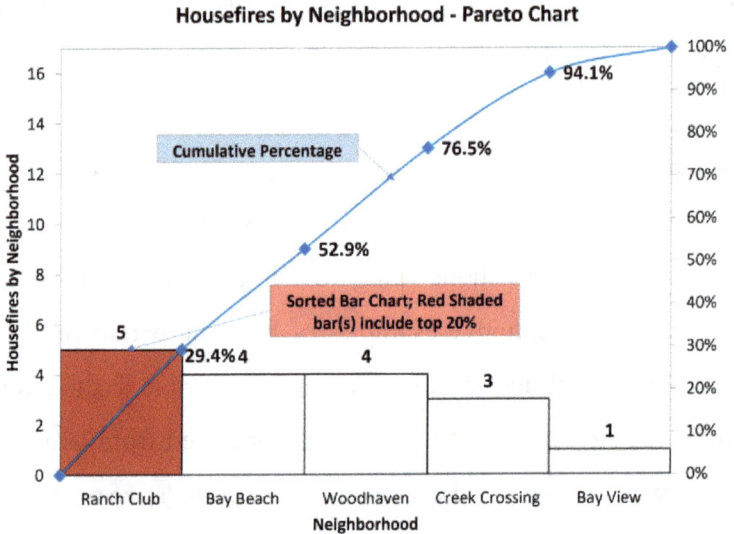

Housefires by Neighborhood - Pareto Chart

The chart has a simple interpretation, focus on addressing the bars that compose at least the top 20%. This is where 80% of your problems are coming from, so focus on improving these issues first. Using Figure 4 as an example, the Ranch Club neighborhood would be the recommended focus for fire prevention activities because at 29.4% this neighborhood meets the threshold of the top 20% of housefires. The only limitation of using this principle within the fire service surrounds data collection. In order to create a pareto chart you need data to quantify the issues. So, if you don't have any data quantifying the problem, a data collection plan may need to be developed first to quantify the problem.

Fishbone Diagram

The last root cause analysis tool is a fishbone diagram (also known as Ishikawa or cause and effect diagram). The aim of this tool is to organize all the causes of a problem through subdivision of categories. The most basic categories include People, Method, Machine, and Material (other categories can be added as needed). The People category includes any causes related to personnel or human resources. The Method category includes any causes related to the process of converting inputs into outputs. The Machine category includes any causes related to electronics, equipment, or information technology. The Material category includes causes that relate to raw materials or supplies. This tool is utilized by first labeling the long spine as the problem. Each of the four categories are then placed along a long branch off the spine. Then, individual causes are included off each of the relevant categories as even smaller branches. One tactic that can be used to help generate discussion is to use a dry-erase board for the fishbone diagram. This makes the image large enough to use post-it notes, where each member going around the room can be encouraged to add a cause to the board. Once the diagram is populated with causes and contributing factors, solutions can be developed to address these areas. Implementation of these solutions should be facilitated using the B.U.R.N. Model (Ch. 8). Figure 9 gives an example of a fishbone diagram.

Figure 9. Fishbone Example

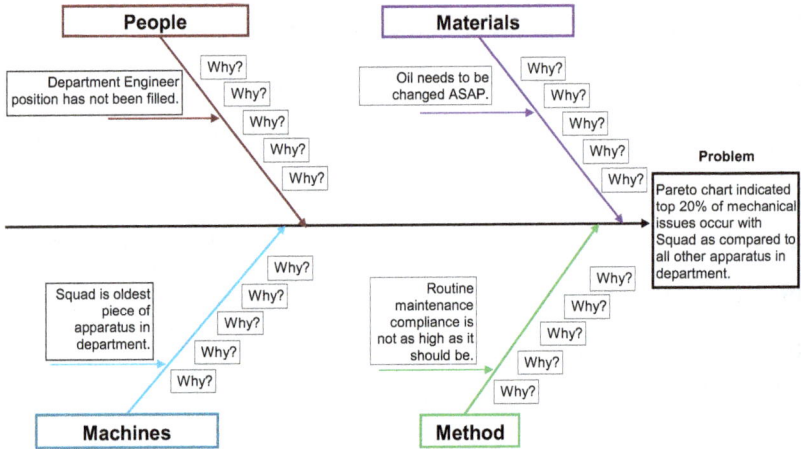

The example given encompasses apparatus mechanical issues. The example leverages a pareto as a starting point, that indicates the Squad as the piece of apparatus with the most mechanical issues. Various causes are then attributed to each of the main categories. The example fishbone diagram shows how a pareto can be incorporated in the problem statement, and how the 5 Why's could be used under each category as a way to further drill down if needed. The fishbone diagram is a great way to organize and incorporate a comprehensive root cause analysis.

Lean Waste

It can sometimes be difficult to brainstorm various causes and issues that populate the fishbone diagram. One methodology that can be utilized to inspire and uncover root causes is Lean. Lean improvement was developed by Toyota, and champions efficiency and the elimination of waste in a process. In this instance, waste is defined as any activity that does not add value to the customer. Lean categorizes waste into eight categories: defects, inventory, motion, overproduction, over processing, transportation, waiting, and human capital. Defects are any waste of effort or resource committed to creating a flawed product or service. An example of this waste might include not positioning a Ladder Truck correctly at the AB corner on a first due fire, and then having to reposition. Or not checking for overhead obstructions when throwing a ladder, having the ladder get hung up on a tree branch, and having to reposition and re-throw the ladder again. These are defects. Inventory is the waste of inefficient storing of supplies, spoilage beyond expiration, or having excess. This could include having medications expire on ambulances, or fuel going bad that's stored for running saws. The waste of motion is any movement by a person that is in excess of what is absolutely needed. Wasted motion might occur on a cardiac arrest if the positions of compression, AFD, and ventilation aren't delineated, and wasted motion could occur at the transition of roles at the end of each cycle. Overproduction waste is associated with producing more than what is needed or producing something too early. This could include loading a patient into an ambulance that hasn't been cleaned yet, or not breaking the line when deploying the bumper line on a vehicle fire and laying out too much hose that needs extra time and effort to flake out. Over processing is the waste of having too many steps in a process or being overly detailed. An example of this may include giving a long and overly detailed return to command when asked for a status check, instead of giving a C.A.N. report. Transportation waste is the unnecessary movement of resources, materials, or patients. An example might be having to run back-and-forth to the Squad for tools on a vehicle extrication as they are needed instead of bringing the tools all at once in the easily accessible warm zone. Waiting involves the waste associated with a delay before another step can be completed, or anything involving a line. This could manifest in examples like excessive apparatus staging or ambulances waiting to transfer patients to hospitals. The waste associated with human capital involves staff that are unmotivated, have low engagement, or are unsupported. Examples of this might include overqualified individuals not being utilized to their full potential, burnout, or staff injuries. When there is difficulty in filling out a fishbone diagram, thinking of these various waste categories can help uncover issues that might not be readily apparent and allows for the ability to dig deeper into a process.

Chapter Summary

In order to improve a process, you first need to identify the problem. A root cause analysis can assist in identifying what is truly causing the problem and help those investigating the issue to focus their efforts on the critical drivers as opposed to symptoms and prevent wasteful improvement efforts. This method helps to ensure sustainable solutions as opposed to failed interventions that require further expenditure of time and resources to perform the rework needed to analyze the situation again. Fix it right the first time with a root cause analysis. The root cause analysis section relates to the Efficiency value of V.I.P.E.R. as it seeks to identify the causes of waste, and also seeks to eliminate contributing causes for broken processes which relates to the value of Variance Inhibiting.

Chapter 6: Human Resources and Motivation Management

As an officer or leader in your department, how do you manage your members? Do you do what comes naturally, or replicate what you have seen others do? Have you actually stopped and considered how impactful your management style is? Do you have a plan, or do you just wing it? Management of others is often difficult and can be quite overwhelming at times. To help with this it's best to have a plan or framework to rely on. This is referred to as a strategic human resource plan, where you think critically about the management of others, and operate within a plan to both respond to issues and to motivate others. When you show up on scene, everyone has their assignments based on SOG's/SOP's. In the same way, having a plan about how you want to manage others can help add clarity to your actions and help you act more prepared as opposed to a "deer in the headlights". This chapter encapsulates the internal channel of the V.I.P.E.R. model.

Member Categories

Leading and managing a department at its core is the management of the motivation for its members to maximize their effort and impact. To accomplish this one should employ a strategic mindset. Pynes and Lombardi (2012) outline a practical and effective model in their text *Human Resources Management for Health Care Organizations: A Strategic Approach*. The authors discuss the use of a Performance Matrix. This matrix divides your membership into groups, and then outlines specific motivations and actions to manage each of these groups. The groups within the Performance Matrix are superstars, steadies, and nonplayers. Within a department, superstars make up around 10%-20% of members, steadies are 60%-70%, and nonplayers are 10%-15% (see the chapter on Control Charts to understand why this distribution isn't random).

Superstars

Superstars are those individuals who exhibit outstanding performance and who flourish with change, seeing change not as a threat but as an opportunity. They have also gained the respect of their peers and are sought out for assistance and mentorship due to their exemplary skills and abilities. Superstars are excellent change agents, who are early adopters to new initiatives, and often propose new and innovative solutions themselves. Going the extra mile is a baseline expectation for them.

Steadies

Steadies make up the majority of the workforce; they are reliable and solid in their work. Some steadies may have a high level of expertise in a specific area and meet expectations in their remaining duties. Pynes and Lombardi (2012) argue that within this category of steadies are five subcategories of members as well. (1)

Hidden superstars are steadies with the potential of becoming a superstar with the right mentorship and coaching. Think of a bright rising member of the department who is hungry for more responsibility and the opportunity to prove themselves. (2) Technical superstars are highly proficient in a specialization, but with no managerial duties. Think of a member that is highly proficient in something like technical rescue, yet who is not an officer. (3) Steadies for life reliably meet expectations but don't seek out the responsibilities of management. Think of the wagon driver you can always count on to get the piece out at 3am and is happy in this role. (4) Escalator-gravitaters will throttle their effort based on the circumstance or work being done. Think of the member with great potential that shows glimpses of great work on scene, but who also might shrug off filling out reports. Lastly, (5) borderline nonplayers are barely squeaking by on their duties. Think of the member who does the bare minimum or won't actively help others at the station unless directed. This is the person who watches others racking hose with their arms folded and will only chip in when asked to do so.

According to Pynes and Lombardi (2012) steadies are the largest opportunity for a manager, not only because they represent the largest proportion of a workforce, but because steadies can be swayed to become either a superstar or a nonplayer depending on the circumstances. If they are mentored and offered development, they can become a superstar. If they are not coached adequately, they can be influenced by the negative attributes of nonplayers and become nonplayers themselves.

Nonplayers

Nonplayers are the smallest proportion of a workforce yet demand the most attention as the most problematic group. The pareto principle is seen here as well, where 80% of a manager's time and attention are taken by only 20% of the most problematic members. The authors describe this group as agitators, which is an accurate descriptor. They stir hostility within the department through such methods as gossip or spiteful words. Pynes and Lombardi (2012) conclude that nonplayers develop bitterness towards leadership "in particular by their lackluster work performance, constant questioning of work objectives, and inappropriate challenges to authority" (p. 53).

Strategic Human Resources Management Situations by Group Motivation

Now that we have identified the various groups of members within a department, the next step is to understand how to manage and motivate each of these groups accordingly. Pynes and Lombardi (2012) propose several problems that may arise with these groups, and how to address them:

☒ Issue: Nonplayers may misrepresent their feelings as the majority. Typically steadies, the largest group, are quiet and content with their work and so won't contradict an outspoken nonplayer. And a superstar may understand their role as a non-manager, and feel it isn't their place to correct such behavior.

 ✓ Solution: Promote the views of the steadies and superstars to drown-out the complaining of the nonplayers. Use such devices as asking superstars/steadies to speak-up during group forums or conduct and display internal survey results proving that the nonplayer's perspective is in fact the minority and not representative of the group as a whole.

☒ Issue: Nonplayers allow their personal issues to affect both their work, and the work of others. Their behavioral issues and traits become a large irritation for other members of the department and their officers, which can cause aggravation in the station or on scene.

 ✓ Solution: Split these behavioral issues into two groups: those that are unpleasant personality traits that simply must be dealt with, and those that can have a harmful impact on operations or on patient safety. Tolerate the former and document the latter as evidence for future remedial action.

☒ Issue: Steadies or nonplayers don't want to progress or cannot accept change. Steadies may be content with the status quo for how "things used to be" or "the way we have always done this," and nonplayers may not want to put forth any extra effort.

  ✓ Solution: Employ superstars as change agents to help champion the change. Also, provide effective information to the holdouts that proves a problem exists, creates a burning platform, and provides the plan for how to fix it. (See B.U.R.N. model in change management chapter)

☒ Issue: Nonplayers will harp and overstate on everything that is wrong with the department, weakening morale. The superstars and steadies are typically too well-mannered to correct them.

  ✓ Solution: Systematically call out accomplishments and gains made by the department, which will both dilute the statements made by the nonplayer, and act as motivation and recognition for the hard work completed by steadies and superstars.

- ☒ Issue: When a new change is being made (technique, tool, policy, SOG, etc.), the nonplayer will only comment on all the ways it could fail. This can stir doubt among the steadies.

  - ✓ Solution: Challenge the nonplayer to offer a better solution or plan instead of only giving negative remarks. If they cannot, move forward with the proposed plan.

- ☒ Issue: When you give a task (at the station, not on scene), a nonplayer may ignore or misrepresent your directions. In some cases, they may alter the directions to fit their alibi, or even state the directions were never given.

  - ✓ Solution: When delegating tasks, follow-up in writing using email or text. Include the due date, resources that can be used, and a brief idea of what you expect as a finished product. For the nonplayer, this will hold them accountable as they cannot dispute not having received the information. For superstars, this provides the opportunity to exceed expectations and provides documentation they can use for positive performance reviews. For example, if an officer is directed to change out all the attack lines on the wagon by Friday, they can get it done by Wednesday if they wish to exceed expectations.

☒ Issue: Some nonplayers have to be continually reminded on how to execute their duties. This could be the member who after being shown multiple times still forgets how to rerack the crosslays, as an example. On scene this person lacks the ability to make decisions, cannot act swiftly, and draws the time and attention from others as they are trying to do their own job. This person might then blame others, management, or a host of other reasons (none of which include themselves) for the deficiency. This could be a result of a lack of skills or a lack of adjustment to the department's management style.

   ✓ Solution: Instill confidence for those with a skill deficiency, which is usually achieved through repetition. Encouragement is the key. For others who continue to need constant direction even after retraining, document their infractions as evidence for remedial actions.

☒ Issue: Business meetings, board meetings, or officer meetings can quickly come off the rails when a nonplayer takes over and steers it towards a critique or gripe session. Pynes and Lombardi (2012) describe it nicely, "as experts on 'everything that went wrong,' nonplayers are very qualified to conduct this session, particularly when they are presented with an open forum" (p. 70). They can effectively take your meeting hostage as a platform to pontificate on all their perceived problems.

- ✓ Solution: The key to avoiding this is to hold tight reins on the meeting. This can be done using an agenda with timeframes for each topic and/or speaker. Also, redirect the conversation back to the topic at hand, for instance, "I understand you may have concerns, but right now we are discussing X, and can address your concerns after the meeting."

Positive and Negative Reinforcement

Both positive and negative reinforcement can be utilized for motivation, although the weighted distribution should lean towards the positive as opposed to the negative. Since superstars thrive on positive reinforcement, this should be utilized as the main management style for this group. Support, development, and recognition give energy to superstars that motivate them to give extra effort and to take the initiative. Steadies also benefit from positive reinforcement, as it gives them reassurance that they are doing the right thing. Examples of positive reinforcement might include providing praise or rewards for positive behaviors or accomplishments, granting of additional responsibilities, incentives, or benefits, allowance for more autonomy, providing learning/development opportunities, or acknowledging someone's hard work with a simple "good job, thanks for your help."

Negative reinforcement should be used sparingly. An example of appropriate use might include getting someone's attention on scene because conditions are rapidly changing, or they are doing something unsafe. In this case being assertive and overly direct is warranted. Also, Pynes and Lombardi (2012) advise that negative reinforcement should be reserved for nonplayers, who will need strict oversight, documentation of infringements, and performance improvement plans. These actions would be considered *productive* negative reinforcement. *Unproductive* negative reinforcement would include actions such as belittling in front of others, yelling, berating, and exclusion. Micromanaging is another form of unproductive negative reinforcement. The officer that micromanages is one that, for one reason or another, does not trust their crew and so feels the need to oversee every detail and babysit. While the officer may feel that they have more control, what they don't realize is this will create an unhealthy over-reliance on them as members of the crew will not be able to make decisions for themselves or grow. The crew members will eventually feel suffocated and symptoms of burnout will begin to develop.

Negative reinforcement may yield *some* results in certain situations in the short term, but will eventually erode the morale of your department if used in excess. This decline in morale will grow quickly and exponentially, causing the eroded morale to fracture and buckle your department. You may see tangible repercussions of this, such as: lack of participation (such as in drills or staffing for fundraising events), increased symptoms of burnout, visible and more frequent confrontations and shouting between members that typically wouldn't occur, and most fundamentally a lack of members putting forth extra effort or going the extra mile. Prolific use of negative reinforcement is the cornerstone of a weak leader. It takes empathy, commitment, and critical thinking to provide positive reinforcement to members in an effort to help them reach their full potential through coaching and mentoring. The constant exposure of a person's flaws without advice or a plan for improvement is a recipe for disaster for a department.

Reinforcement Example

As an example, you may find this situation during a hotwash after a call. Leaders may take this opportunity to correct behavior and actions, and rightly so. However, the manner in which this is conducted is critical in determining the mettle of a leader. Poor leadership will put their officers and other crew members "on blast" in front of each other, calling out every mistake and flaw. A strong leader will applaud the positives from the call, highlighting certain things individual members or the crew as a whole did well. The strong leader will then correct or highlight any improvements needed in the collective using the plural "we", "the team", or "our department" as examples. This way members aren't singled out in front of the each other. If there are errors that need to be fixed or addressed with an individual member or officer from the call, then they would be pulled aside out of sight and earshot of the rest of the membership. When this conversation occurs and the issues are identified, it's imperative that the "why" be communicated. Telling the member "why" something is wrong is paramount for building understanding, which is the foundation that learning and improvement is built upon. Sometimes the conversation will end after the leader critiques the member, but this would be premature. The most important part of the discussion is the plan regarding how the member can fix the issue to ensure improvement. Without it, expect the issue to continue to occur, because the leader hasn't provided the member with a plan forward. This process is the hallmark of a strong and motivational leader that values, and is invested in, the continued development of his/her department. These examples highlight certain key and classic HR elements: praise in public while criticizing in private and reinforcing the positive.

Chapter Summary

Understanding what drives and motivates an individual is key to managing and leading them. In order to improve the efficiency of one's crew, utilizing the correct motivational technique is important to maximizing their potential. Over-reliance on any one motivational technique (especially negative) in a one-size-fits-all managerial attitude will only work on some staff, while isolating many others. The fire and EMS service need leaders that take the time to understand them, and are then dedicated enough to manage and coach them in a way that allows them to reach their full potential.

Dr. David Hupp

Chapter 7: Marketing and Forecasting

Marketing is a critical element within a fire and EMS department yet is often overlooked. Further, typical quality improvement models do not include a marketing element. However, because of the unique need that volunteer fire and EMS departments have, the V.I.P.E.R. Improvement Model includes the marketing element in the external channel to address recruitment of new volunteer members, fundraising, and creating a positive relationship with the community. Both my Bachelors and Masters business degrees have marketing concentrations, and I have found these skills very useful in developing plans for my volunteer department.

Strategic Marketing Plan: 5P's and 3C's

There is a common misconception that nonprofits such as fire departments or hospitals don't need finances. Being a nonprofit just means that part of its earnings don't have to be paid to the government, whereas for-profit organizations don't get this tax-exempt status and therefore have to pay the applicable taxes. Because of this, fire and EMS departments still need to perform fundraising to make ends meet. This brings the concept of marketing to the forefront. In addition to fundraising, other utilizations of marketing for a department can include recruitment for volunteer departments and establishing a positive relationship with the community and other stakeholders. Another misconception is that marketing is advertising. While this is correct, marketing encompasses much more than just advertising. Marketing is the communication of a company's product or service to garner business. In order to accomplish this, a strategic marketing plan identifies what the department offers, who its customers are, and what the department is competing against. A strategic marketing plan should include the 5P's and the 3C's.

The 5P's

The 5P's stands for Product, Price, Promotion, Place, and People. The Product category stands for the product or service that the organization offers. This section should include all the specifications and characteristics of the product or service. Be specific. The Price is what it costs for the customer to buy the product or service. As an example, a department might review the fundraising patterns for a mail-based fundraiser. How many donations did the department receive as compared to last year? Has the average contribution amount gone up or down? This section can also include the cost of various items, such as the cost of postage for the mail-based fundraiser, or the breakeven point that needs to be surpassed for the cost of a specialized mailer design. Promotion is the section dedicated to your traditional advertising, which includes how an organization is communicating with their customer.

This could include websites, search engine boosting, billboards, social media, newspaper/magazines, radio, etc. As social media has taken over as a vital platform, a good rule of thumb is to limit posts to 150 characters if possible, include an image or video along with the text to catch attention, post on weekdays between 9 am and 3 pm, and include a call to action with time sensitivity by starting with an action word followed by urgency, such as "volunteer today" or "donate now" for example. Place is where the business transaction takes place. As an example, does fundraising take place out in the community through such devices as a boot drive, or are donations generated online? The People section is focused on your members or staff. This can include their training, certifications, staff engagement or burnout levels, or other pertinent human resource concepts.

The 3C's

The 3C's stands for Customer, Company, and Competitors. The Customer section is dedicated to the profile of an organization's customers. This could include demographics, their needs or wants, their dislikes, and their motivations. The Company section identifies the organization's culture, strengths and weaknesses, and their core competency. This section can be populated with a department's SWOT analysis from their strategic plan. An organization's core competency is simply what the company does exceptionally well.

This could include a department that has a specialization in confined space rescue or is fortunate enough to have a varied and well-maintained fleet of apparatus. The last section is Competitors, which is an analysis of the competitive environment. While this may be more difficult to conceptualize initially from a nonprofit organizational view (one department isn't exactly competing against another to take care of a patient), it can help if one broadens their scope. In thinking from a recruitment standpoint, the competition may be the time and demands the volunteer would otherwise have with their family, working, or other leisure activities.

Marketing Examples

In order to gain better understanding, let's look at two specific examples and how marketing can help. The general process should occur as follows:

- Identify what your department does exceptionally well (*core competency*).

- Determine how to promote this in a way that is different (*differentiation*) from what is currently offered (*competitive advantage*) elsewhere either in the community or other departments (*marketing position*).

- Craft a message (*promotion*) that is then delivered to the customer (*target market*).

- Deliver this message to the target in a way that gains their attention and business (*advertising*).

In this first example, let's consider a department that is creating a strategic marketing plan to recruit more members to its department. Also, this department completed a strategic plan and SWOT, and identified one strength is their training. The department has a robust training program, and acts as a magnet station that even other departments seek training from. The second example is a marketing strategy that outlines the key marketing tactic of cross-branding. This involves creating a partnership with another organization to leverage each other's unique strengths and realize marketing gains that each organization would otherwise not be able to accomplish alone.

Example 1: Recruitment Marketing Plan. Goal: Recruit new members (increase membership by 5%) to the department through renewed and innovative marketing tactics aimed at purposeful and effective exposure towards the community by the end of this year. Product:

- Our department does an exceptional job at offering training opportunities for our members and community. This translates to a proficient first responder membership, in addition to continued growth and learning opportunities. Specifically, we have a number of members who are also trained as Fire/EMS Instructors and CPR Instructors. Frequent training classes have been offered at our station over the past several years, and our CPR program is robust and offers both our membership and community training.

- Differentiation, Competitive Advantage, Marketing Position: While training classes are offered throughout the region, ours is unique in that it can (and has) offered many classes at our station as host. Our CPR program has equipment and a trailer for a robust teaching delivery system that not every department is fortunate to have.

Price:

- Typically, the department covers training costs for members. The only cost to the member is the time and energy needed to attend classes, which can be difficult when trying to work within a busy schedule.

Promotion:

- Create a social media campaign that reaches the community in an effort to notify, educate, and recruit.
    - Social Media Post: Include picture of all instructors together in front of apparatus. Include the number of instructors, number of classes held over the past 3 years, drill information (3-4 drills a month, sample of topics).

- o Provide a recurring theme of posts each week highlighting any classes or drills held, with pictures showing what participants are doing.

Place:

- The department has a classroom that can host up to 30 students, with a projector and other multimedia devices. The department also has a training prop, forcible entry door, vehicle extrication area, and confined space maze.

People:

- The department membership includes six training instructors certified to teach the state-certified classes, as well as nine CPR instructors.

Customer:

- The target market would include those that may be hesitant to join due to a lack of experience. Our department has the resources to teach the knowledge, skills, and abilities needed. Further, if anyone that does have experience and would like to grow and take their skills to the next level, our department can offer that opportunity.

Company:

- The volunteer department has 75 active members and is located in a suburb of a major metropolitan city. The department has both fire and EMS personnel, with two ambulances, squad, truck, wagon, and tanker. The department excels and has a robust training program as a strength. The weakness lies in the limited number of members available to keep up with the growing call volume, which has grown by 15% over the past 5 years.

Competition:

- The competition for the prospective member lies in competing with time and priorities. The department is located in a bedroom community, that commutes into the city for work. This creates a very hectic commute, giving little time for commuting workers to spend with their families. This makes finding time to volunteer at the department a challenge. In conducting a field survey of people attending the last open house event, many people believed the training would be prohibitive in time. It was determined that showcasing the in-house training program might alleviate these concerns, as they wouldn't have to travel to the regional training center but could gain all the training and certifications required at the station.

Example 2: Preplan Cross Branding Marketing Plan. Goal: Add 50 preplans within 12 months.

Product:

- A preplan is a document that helps a fire department proactively assess a company or building with respect to physical layout, occupancy, contact information, response tactics, water supply, hazards, and other considerations. It helps to improve tactical response, improve scene safety, and reduce the need for forcible entry if owners can be contacted. Preplans also have an effect on a region's ISO (Insurance Services Office) rating.

Price:

- There is typically no monetary cost for a building owner to have a preplan done. A cost of time is needed by a fire department to conduct the preplan. In addition, software products exist that help to create more robust preplans that can be recalled digitally.

Place:

- A preplan is conducted on-site and is either completed and kept on paper in a binder, or digitally using a software package.

Promotion:

- Awareness Campaign – Build awareness of pre-plan purpose and mitigate/dispel negative assumptions and improve preplan participation.
    - o Deliver presentations to Business Association, Civic Association, and select businesses 1-on-1.
        - Develop a Powerpoint presentation with the focus of explaining what a preplan is, and what it isn't. Discuss the purpose of a preplan regarding how it improves response through preparation. Additionally, outline the elements of a preplan and share the actual preplan document for transparency. Explain the benefits of the preplan such as a reduction in property destruction or loss and improving their ISO rating, which can lower their insurance premiums.
        - Develop an FAQ brochure for passive marketing as a leave-behind for individual businesses.
- Partnership Program – Develop and implement a partnership program that highlights a business's willingness to participate in the preplan process and support the

community. Cross-branding with a nonprofit can add several benefits for a business. Reputation: goodwill can be built for a business when it is seen alongside a nonprofit and their respective altruistic cause, which can impact the business's reputation and perception of increased accountability and integrity. This can develop loyalty in both customers and employees. Outcome: a symbiotic relationship is created as the department gets more preplans and the business gets cross-branding benefits.

- o Create branding logo.
  - ▪ Special logo that retains elements of the fire department while incorporating the essence of partnership.
  - ▪ Develop into a window sticker for business to proudly display that they have participated in a preplan.
- o Create a social media package that posts a story on the department's social media page which highlights the business's participation. Crosswalk this with the business's own social media page if they are willing.

People:

- The department has several officers with experience in conducting preplans with businesses.

Customer:

- Businesses may have some hesitancy to participate in a preplan program. Some may see this as an inspection, fearing the fire department will penalize their business with violations.

Company:

- The department identified in its strategic plan that a goal was to increase its relationship with the community. It also identified a strategic value as improving firefighter safety. The tactic of preplans satisfy both these items, hence the goal of increasing the number of preplans.

Competition:

- The competition that the fire department is facing is competing with the perception of negative business outcomes (violations or business closures) as a result of participating in the preplan.

Forecasting

Forecasting is a marketing concept that can assist a fire department in planning and allocation of resources. Organizations may forecast future year's revenues, expenses, in addition to many other metrics. A department may find forecasting useful during budgeting time, when a department will need to project and anticipate any costs for the upcoming year. Forecasting can help provide an estimate or frame of reference that has the unique ability to reduce the impact of any previous years' extreme highs or lows (outliers), and provide a more reasonable expectation for what might occur based on what has happened in the past. This leads to several critical disclaimers. The first is this: forecasts are always wrong. This might sound like great reason why *not* to use it, allow for some explanation. When one looks at the weather forecast for tomorrow, maybe it states it will be 80 degrees, 41% humidity, and mostly cloudy. The weather actually ends up with a high of 82 degrees, 45% humidity, and partly cloudy. Technically the forecast was wrong. However, most people would agree that the forecast was pretty accurate in projecting the conditions of temperature, humidity, and cloud cover, which was accurate enough to not need any daily plans to be altered as a result. This brings up another critical concept, which is error rate or margin of error. The usefulness of a forecast is dependent upon its margin of error. Another good rule of thumb with forecasting is that they will lose accuracy as you forecast further into the future, as well as the narrower the geography. As an example, a forecast looking five years in the future will generally be more accurate than a ten-year projection. Also, projecting call volume for the combined departments in a county will be more accurate than projecting call volume for an individual department.

Forecasting Model Types

There are many different forecasting methods, however two of the most manageable are moving average (MA) and weighted moving average (WMA). There are others such as exponential and linear regression, but for the purposes of this text we will review only the MA and WMA. The MA is simply taking an average of data points to project the next one. As an example, let's use a three-year MA evaluating call volume. So, use the average of years 2021, 2022, and 2023 to forecast year 2024. The "moving" part of moving average means for year 2025 you would just move up the years and then average 2022, 2023, and 2024. The WMA uses the same premise but allows you to add weights to the years so one can add more weight to recent years. For example, using 20% for year 2021, 30% for 2022, and 50% for 2023 to calculate a forecast for year 2024 (the % total weights must add to 100%). This method applies more weight to recent years as a way to apply greater relevancy towards recent events. The weights for each year are up to the user's discretion.

Forecasting Accuracy

One simple way to evaluate the accuracy of a model is through testing. One can calculate each model, and then plot them against the actual performance to see which one tracks closer. For example, if you have 10 years' worth of data, you can use the first three years to calculate the MA and WMA and continue moving each year with the new forecast. Then, place them on a line graph together to see which one has the smallest variance to the actual performance. A department can also use statistical measures such as mean absolute percentage error (MAPE) to evaluate accuracy. Here is the calculation for the MAPE: (Absolute Value (actual – forecast) / actual) x 100. Essentially you take the actual performance value then subtract the forecasted value. This number is converted to the absolute value, meaning if it is a negative number, make it positive. Next, divide this number by the actual performance value. Lastly, multiply this number by 100 to make it a percentage. Practically, this tells you how far away the forecast is from the actual value. For example, if the MAPE was 5% then the forecast deviates by 5% from what actually occurred. The smaller the number, the more accurate the forecast. One then takes the average of all the individual MAPE scores for an overall score. An advantage of the WMA model is the weight percentages for each year can be changed, and then tested in different combinations to yield a lower MAPE score, and thus a more accurate model.

Forecast Example

Let's use these models to project call volume using the past 10 years' worth of incident call data as an example. See Figure 10 for the data, and calculations for both MA and WMA, using a rolling

3 years of data each. Notice the weights for the WMA were set at 10% for year 1, 20% for year 2, and 70% for year 3.

Figure 10. Incident Forecast Table

Year	Actual Incidents	3 Year Moving Average	Weighted Moving Average (10%, 20%, 70%)	3 Yr. MA MAPE (%)	WMA MAPE (%)
Year 1	632			Formula: (ABS(Actual-Forcast)/Actual) x 100	Formula: (ABS(Actual-Forcast)/Actual) x 100
Year 2	720	Formula: Average Year 1, 2, 3 for Year 4...	Formula: (0.1*Year 1)+(0.2*Year 2)+(0.7*Year 3) = Year 4...		
Year 3	1119				
Year 4	1214	824	991	32.2%	18.4%
Year 5	1271	1018	1146	19.9%	9.9%
Year 6	1468	1201	1244	18.2%	15.2%
Year 7	1508	1318	1403	12.6%	6.9%
Year 8	1363	1416	1476	3.9%	8.3%
Year 9	1404	1446	1403	3.0%	0.1%
Year 10	1452	1425	1406	1.9%	3.2%
Year 11	Forecast	1406	1434	*13.1%	*8.9%

*average of above individual MAPE Scores

Based on the above information, see Figure 11 to show a graphical representation of the models in comparison to the actual number of incidents for each individual year.

Figure 11. Forecast Model Comparison Graph

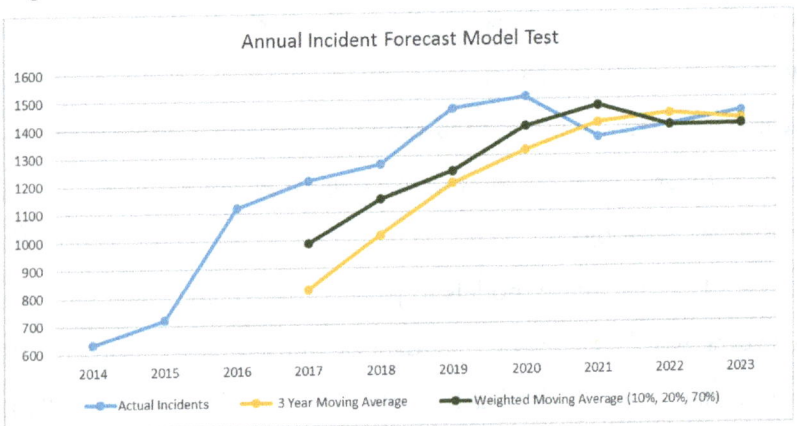

Using Figure 11, you can see that the WMA model seems to track slightly closer to the actual performance over time, so this would be the best model to use in this situation. This is reinforced by viewing the error rate MAPE score, which shows the WMA model (8.9%) as having a lower error rate than the MA model (13.1%). Therefore, the WMA model would be the best choice as it is the more accurate of the two models. Thus, for year 11 the projected number of incidents would be 1434, or a decline of -1.24% from the previous year. A department could use this information to project an allocation of resources and make decisions for the next year. The department could make an assumption that the number of incidents should remain relatively similar to last year, with the chance for a very slight decrease of approximately 1%.

Chapter Summary

A strategic marketing plan is an excellent exercise for a fire or EMS department to conduct in order to maximize their exposure and to control the message being delivered. This is critical for volunteer departments seeking membership and fundraising dollars. Forecasting is a useful technique that can help to mitigate the risk of a department by strategically allocating resources in a proactive (instead of reactive) manner. These relate to the Variance Inhibiting values of the V.I.P.E.R. model as they seek to reduce the amount of risk or variance for the department. Marketing and forecasting also seek to achieve the goals set forth by the strategic plan, which coincides with the Performance value of V.I.P.E.R. as well.

Chapter 8: Change Management using the B.U.R.N. Model

Within the V.I.P.E.R. Improvement Model, each of the three channels converge on the Change Management section. This is due to the fact that the outcome for each channel will yield some type of improvement or solution that will need to be implemented in a change. The concept of change management is the practice of thinking critically and planning how a change will occur to promote its sustainment. Change can be difficult for some individuals, as they have apprehension for the unknown, their job security, or in their ability to succeed in a new environment. Thus, many times a change in a process can have false starts or even failure if buy-in isn't established correctly. The nonplayers may actively petition against it, and others may roll their eyes and just return to the old process after a certain amount of time has passed. Other reasons changes might fail are because changes are over-simplified and fail to give enough attention to detail, leaders underestimate the degree of resistance to the change, the change occurs too quickly for people to absorb or understand, expectations and accountability are not established, not enough training opportunities are given to learn the new change, or individuals feel that the change is impressed upon them without their input. In order to address these pitfalls, I have created a change management framework that is developed specifically for the fire and EMS service, which provides a guide to help instill a positive atmosphere around a solution to promote its compliance and sustainment. This framework is known as the B.U.R.N. Change Management Model (Figure 12). B.U.R.N. stands for Burning Platform, Urgency through Action, Requirements for Change, and Need for Sustainment.

B.U.R.N. Model Steps

Figure 12. B.U.R.N. Change Management Model

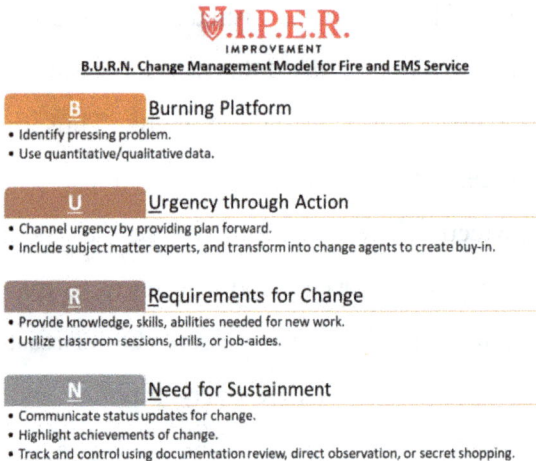

V.I.P.E.R.
IMPROVEMENT
B.U.R.N. Change Management Model for Fire and EMS Service

B | Burning Platform
- Identify pressing problem.
- Use quantitative/qualitative data.

U | Urgency through Action
- Channel urgency by providing plan forward.
- Include subject matter experts, and transform into change agents to create buy-in.

R | Requirements for Change
- Provide knowledge, skills, abilities needed for new work.
- Utilize classroom sessions, drills, or job-aides.

N | Need for Sustainment
- Communicate status updates for change.
- Highlight achievements of change.
- Track and control using documentation review, direct observation, or secret shopping.

Burning Platform

The first step involves creating a burning platform with a review of data (quantitative such as metrics or control charts, or qualitative such as compelling examples of past incidents, patient complaints, or community responses) for the current situation and how the department is not meeting a goal or failing to meet an expectation. This step needs to show why there is a problem, and therefore a need for change.

Urgency Through Action

The next step involves building urgency for action with a path forward. After the initial step of justifying why a change is needed, the next obvious question is "ok what do we do now?", "how do we fix it?" At this point the department channels the urgency for a plan forward by outlining the solution or action plan. A valuable tactic in this step is to involve those who will be actively participating in the change, or subject matter experts, in its development to increase the compliance of the new change. This is due to two reasons. First, a department can expect a larger acceptance for a change, and a greater compliance level, if those who will be expected to actually perform the newly changed process are involved in its development. Second, the individuals involved in this creation process will develop pride in this new change as they had a hand in its development and were asked to be included, which can transform them into change agents as they will look to promote the change when management isn't around and provide positive word of mouth. The principle is that they will feel a greater amount of pride that they participated in creating the solution, and therefore will be more likely to use the new process. Also, subject matter experts have the most amount of detailed knowledge regarding the process, and therefore should be consulted. As an example, it might be a good idea to run a new water rescue SOG by a department that runs these types of calls frequently. Once a department enlists subject matter experts and communicates the proposed solution and the path forward, move on to the next step.

Requirements for Change

The next step is the requirements for change, which includes the training of knowledge, skills, and abilities needed for the new process or solution. This can include actual classroom sessions, drills, or job-aids (checklists, reminders, FAQ's, contact information for questions) to assist with the new change, both in preparation and in real-time. It's important to give the opportunity for practical exercise as well, so that muscle memory and tacit knowledge can be built up.

Need for Sustainment

The last step is fulfilling the need for sustainment of the change. Communication should be delivered well ahead of the actual change in order to give members time to digest the information and to prepare. Multiple reminders using several different modes should be utilized to ensure everyone is on the same page (emails, texts, newsletters, bulletin boards, verbal reminders at staff meetings). Once the change has been implemented, the department should provide frequent communication on updates regarding the change, especially during the early days of the implementation. These updates can include the status of the new process, key metrics showing the impact of the change, and highlighting any accomplishments or achievements of the change to build positivity. Examples of achievements could include meeting milestone targets, a message or bulletin board showing members or staff committing to the change, or a press release/ social media post showing positive impacts with the community. The need for sustainment is also accomplished with a control plan, which is a management plan that ensures the change is being utilized. This could include documentation review (such as quality control of patient care reports or incident reports), direct observations, or secret shopping to make sure the change is being adhered to. This step ensures the change is being hardwired. A control chart can be helpful to identify if a positive shift has occurred, and once achieved, that it is monitored and sustained through investigation if any unfavorable shifts or outliers occur that would indicate a regression backwards.

Change Management Example

Let's use the B.U.R.N. Change Management Model in an example. Suppose in using the V.I.P.E.R. Improvement Model a department included reducing scratch rates as a goal within their strategic plan. In conducting the process control and root cause analysis sections of the quality improvement channel, they identified that the scratch rates are occurring as a result of a lack of department members being at the station to respond to calls, especially during the mid-morning and late evening times. As a result, the group decided that in order to best serve their community, scheduling duty hours is necessary to ensure consistent coverage throughout the day. The group has initially proposed mandating that all members sign up for two six-hour shifts per month, for a total of twelve hours. Now that the improvement has been identified and needs to be implemented, the change management process needs to be employed.

Using the B.U.R.N. model, the first step is *Burning Platform*. To accomplish this, the department presented the scratch rate to the membership at the monthly business meeting using a control chart. The control chart showed the scratch rate trending in the wrong direction, which was confirmed using one of the statistical control chart rules that identified six monthly data points in a row ascending. This created an atmosphere of clarity that this is a pressing issue.

With the burning platform established, the department moved on to the second step, *Urgency through Action*. The question was asked, "OK, what do we do now to get the scratch rates under control?" The second step was executed by providing the action plan forward mandating two six-hour shifts of duty a month.

Additionally, a workgroup was commissioned to vet the new plan, and to develop the finer details of operationalizing it. Using the B.U.R.N. model, the department included several running members in the group (as opposed to just operational or administrative officers) that have various work and family schedules. In this group, it was identified that three-hour shifts would be more manageable. Therefore, the recommendation was made to have four three-hour shifts instead. Pulling the workgroup together with members who would be affected by the new policy was pivotal in uncovering this recommendation. The department might have actually lost members who couldn't stay for six hours at a time, and therefore not meet the commitment needed. This way the total hours are covered as before, but members can cover them in more manageable chunks, making it a win-win situation: hours covered, input taken seriously, and the members felt heard.

With the second step completed, the department moved onto the third step of the B.U.R.N. model, *Requirements for Change*. In this stage members needed to acquire the knowledge of scheduling their duty. So, drill nights for the next two weeks dedicated a portion of the time that focused on showing members how to enter their schedule into the new system.

The fourth and last stage of the B.U.R.N. model, *Need for Sustainment*, was accomplished by sending out reminders of the duty schedule requirement several weeks in advance via email and verbal reminders. After the new schedule went live, the department began reviewing monthly if members were making their hours and following up individually with letters to make them aware they needed to make their hours up, and to offer help if they needed it to catch up (i.e. tracking and controlling). The department also sent a memo to the membership showing their monthly compliance percentage (95%) for members completing their duty hours which fulfilled the communication for change with status updates. The department also showed the impact of this change on the scratch rate at the monthly business meetings using control charts, showing the positive impact duty hours are having on the scratch rate which highlights the achievements.

Chapter Summary

Under the V.I.P.E.R. Improvement Model, change management using the B.U.R.N. model satisfies the Reliability value, which seeks to be consistent, dependable, and accurate. The B.U.R.N. Change Management model provides a step-by-step framework with which to implement a new process or solution that a fire/EMS department has identified. Using this model will help to ensure that the new change is both adhered to and sustainable.

Chapter 9: Risk Management

Risk management is a pivotal part of fire/EMS department leadership. Under the V.I.P.E.R. Improvement model, the Risk Management section sits within the continuous improvement channel. Use this channel if the department is looking to improve on a process that is already working well and is seeking to become even more successful. Typically risk management will occur during a stable period if using a proactive tool, or will occur after an adverse event if using a reactive tool. Once solutions are identified from the Risk Management section, it will cycle back to the Change Management section as the solutions/changes will need to be implemented.

Defining Risk Management

Managing risk can help a department become more financially stable, reduce the amount of negative interactions within a station, and reduce the number of unstable conditions. It's important to attempt to avert a risk from happening in the first place, or if something occurs to mitigate the impact as much as possible. Risk management involves several general strategies: eliminate/avoid the risk, share the risk, or accept the risk (*Risk Analysis and Risk Management*, 2023). In evaluating risk, the department may deem that the risk is simply too high to allow and outweighs the benefits prompting them to eliminate or avoid the situation. This could include allocating a significant amount of company funds to investments tied to the stock market, which might create an unbalanced portfolio, and therefore prompt more diversified options instead. In other situations, sharing the amount of risk involved may be a strategy. This typically involves getting insurance. The department and the insurance company share the risk, where the department pays a premium and deductible, and the insurance company will pay out for a covered event. The last strategy is to accept the risk, which typically occurs when there is no way to prevent the risk, when the cost of a loss is less than insuring against the loss, or when the upside is worth the risk.

Aside from these general strategies, there are two notable tools that can be used to assess risk. This chapter will review those two types of risk management techniques, which are proactive risk assessments (before something happens) and reactive risk assessments (after something happens). The proactive risk assessment will be conducted using a Failure Mode and Effect Analysis (FMEA) and the reactive risk assessment will be conducted using the SAFER Matrix developed by The Joint Commission. Both of these methods are ways to assess risk within a department with the focus applied towards improving operations as an outcome.

Failure Mode and Effects Analysis (FMEA)

The FMEA is a proactive risk assessment which focuses on the potential failure modes within a process, and then assessing each of these failure modes with respect to severity, probability of occurrence, and the ability of the failure mode to be detected. Once this assessment is completed, a Risk Priority Number (RPN) is calculated to rank each of the failure modes against one another with the expectation that those ranked at the top will be the focus for improvement efforts. To start using this tool, a problem needs to first be identified. The problem will need to include something that hasn't happened yet but could happen. Alternatively, an FMEA could be used to pressure-test a new process to identify and avoid pitfalls. The first step is to review the process and list all the steps involved. The next step will involve identifying any possible step within the process that could potentially fail, which should be used to populate a list of these failure modes.

How to Identify Failure Modes

In order to help identify possible failures, *Risk Analysis and Risk Management* (2023) provides several categories of threats to consider. Human threats would include factors such as sickness, getting hurt, or even death. Operational threats would include an interruption to operations, an inability to perform business or run calls, an inability to access resources such as apparatus, or supply chain issues. Reputational threats would include damage to community/patient/staff confidence. Procedural threats could include breakdowns in holding members accountable, stealing such as diversion of medications, or deviations from organizational systems such as not filling out patient care reports timely. Project failures would include over-spending on budgets or untimely completion of tasks. Financial threats could include poorly performing investments, inflation, lack of ability to acquire credit, or economic recession. Technical threats could include cyber-attacks or IT system failures. Natural threats would include pandemics, adverse weather, or natural disaster events. Political threats could include changes in policy by various levels of government, laws, cultural strive/tensions, or tax-related changes.

Failure Mode Scoring

After each of the potential failure modes are listed, these failures will be evaluated by the team based on their severity, probability of occurrence, and the ability of the failure to be detected. Each of these will be scored on a scale from 1-10. For severity, the higher the number the more severe the impact of the failure on operations or safety. For occurrence, the higher the number the higher the probability that the failure might occur. For detection, the higher the number the higher the probability that the failure will occur without being detected, and therefore reach the customer or patient. For each failure the RPN will then be calculated (severity x occurrence x detection). Those failures with the highest RPN scores would then be areas that the department would want to focus on initially with respect to solutions. Of note, the RPN scores are relative. So, there is no defined good or bad score, one has to examine if there are several scores that standout. One tool that can be applied to help in this regard is the pareto chart. Simply take the failure modes with their respective RPN scores and create a pareto chart to show which failure modes constitute the top 20% of the highest RPN scores. This is a unique way to integrate quality improvement tools to help in prioritization.

FMEA Example

Let's use an example to add context for an FMEA. To follow the V.I.P.E.R. Improvement Model, the example would need to be a process that already exists and wants to be probed to see if any fine-tuning or continuous improvement can be found. Alternatively, a brand-new process that has yet to be implemented could be used to develop solutions for potential problems. Suppose a department wants to identify the various ways the current process of the department's annual Open House can fail. The Open House has been a great way for the department to showcase the department, apparatus, and skills to the community it serves. The Open House has built goodwill and fostered a good connection with the community and has also primed greater fundraising amounts throughout the year as donations mention the event specifically. Currently the Open House is a successful event, but in an effort to continuously improve, the department wants to identify failure modes to make the event even more successful and prevent any setbacks. In Figure 13, the department has outlined several failure modes that could have a negative impact on the event.

Figure 13. FMEA – Open House Scenario

Failure Mode and Effects Analysis				
Failure Mode Description	**Severity**	**Probability of Occurrence**	**Detection**	**RPN**
Step in process of failure	(1-10)	(1-10)	(1-10)	S*O*D
Lack of member attendance	10	3	8	240
Food trucks not available	7	4	8	224
Inclement weather (rain)	9	5	3	135
Inclement weather (heat)	7	5	3	105
	1-low, 10-high	*1-low, 10-high*	*1-easy, 10-hard*	
	How severe is the effect to the customer?	*How frequently is this likely to occur?*	*How easy is it to detect?*	

The first failure mode would be a lack of member participation for the event. This would have a critical impact as members are needed to staff the various stations, exhibits, demonstrations, and essentially run the event. Therefore, the highest score of 10 is set. The likelihood of this occurring is low as participation has always been solid, however if something unforeseen such as the flu or Covid were to impact a portion of the membership this sets the score at a 3 (low, but not the lowest). The ability for the department to detect a lack of participation is low, as it is based on the expectation that everyone shows up. However, if members decide not to show up, or many get sick, the department wouldn't know until the day of the event, so a higher score of 8 is set. The RPN for this failure mode is 240 (10x3x8).

The second failure mode is if the scheduled food trucks don't attend the event. This is currently the only source of food for the event and is a great draw. Therefore, a score of 7 is set as a moderately high impact because it might impact the length of time people stay but the event could still go on without the food. It has a moderately low probability (4) of occurrence because the event is also a great supply of business for the food trucks, however the department does not have a contract with the food trucks forcing them to be there and is only based on good-faith. Because there is no contract, the ability to detect if they decided not to show is high as the department wouldn't know until the day of the event, yielding a score of 8. The RPN is 224.

The third failure mode would be having bad weather with rain. This would have a severe impact as rain typically deters crowds and would limit the outdoor activities such as the vehicle extrication drill. Further, the department uses a field for parking, making even those wishing to attend for the indoor festivities having to deal with muddy conditions. The severity score would be a 9. The probability of occurrence would be a 5, as it is either going to rain…or it isn't (50/50). The ability to detect is pretty good as the department can use a weather forecast to determine if it will rain or not, yielding a score of 3. The RPN is 135.

The last failure mode is having a hot day. While not quite as severe as a rain event because the department can use tents, fans, and water stations to help accommodate the weather, this threat can still cause attendees to be uncomfortable and may deter them. This yields a severity score of 7. The probability of occurrence is the same coin flip of a 5 as it occurs in September, and the same weather forecasting yields a detection score of 3. The RPN is 105.

The next step is to rank the failure modes by RPN, which lists the lack of member attendance as the riskiest failure mode, followed by lack of food trucks, rainy inclement weather, and then heat inclement weather. The first priority would be to focus attention and efforts to ensure the department membership attends the event as this is the riskiest failure mode. To discern if the other failure modes warrant this first priority as well, a pareto chart in Figure 14 can help to determine what top 20% signals the first priority. See Figure 14 below and identify the 20% cutoff area.

Figure 14. Open House FMEA RPN Pareto Chart

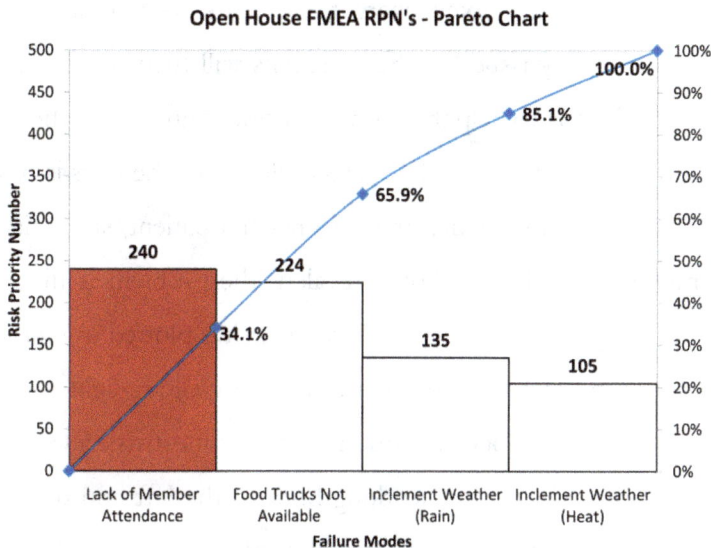

The pareto chart indicates that the top failure mode of lack of member attendance is the only failure mode category in the top 20%, and therefore should be the focus for improvement discussions as 80% of potential problems for the Open House will most likely derive from this category.

SAFER Matrix

The SAFER Matrix is a tool that can assist a department to identify and communicate risks in a condensed graphic. While the FMEA is used proactively to assess risk, the SAFER Matrix balances the equation as being reactive and assessing risks that have already occurred. This risk assessment tool was originally developed for hospitals to use in categorizing safety survey deficiencies (a hospital will have an onsite survey every three years to find any code violations or safety issues). The violations will then be placed on this SAFER Matrix to help the hospital prioritize and assess the risks identified by the surveyors. The categorization of the risks is based on how likely the risk deficiency is to reach a patient/staff/visitor (low, moderate, high) and how prevalent the problem is (limited, pattern, widespread). Based on where the risk is plotted using these two criteria, the matrix employs a heat map (yellow, light orange, dark orange, red) to focus attention on the highest risk levels first (highest in the upper right, working both to the left and down in descending priority). The application of this tool within the fire/EMS service is unique to this book and won't be found elsewhere as it was procured under the permission of The Joint Commission.

SAFER Matrix Example

In order to better understand how the SAFER Matrix can work within your department, let's use an example. Consider a department that has undergone a workplace accident while performing a vehicle extrication. A crew member was performing a lower A-post cut to a vehicle on its side. Once the cut was complete, the vehicle shifted and rolled onto the crew member's hand, pinning the hand to the ground for several seconds until the crew could push the car back just enough for the injured crew member to remove their hand. The injury resulted in several lacerations to the fingers. The SAFER Matrix can help by identifying and prioritizing any risk factors that may have contributed to this incident (risk level to patient/staff/visitor, and problem prevalence/scope). Below are descriptions of the risk factors:

- Rescue struts were not used on this incident to stabilize the vehicle. The only stabilization used were step-chocks. The department typically uses only step-chocks when a vehicle is on its side to save time, with the inclination that this method is enough to prevent a rollover. While this might have been the case, it was just enough for someone's hand to fit under the vehicle. Utilization of tensioned struts on both sides of the vehicle (dirty and clean) may very well have prevented this injury. As this is a critical risk, it is deemed High Risk. Further as this is a department-wide tendency to use only step-chocks, it is also Widespread in scope.

- The injured crew member was performing the cut with both knees on the ground. The department is taught to only go down on one knee so that a quick escape can be made if needed. Trying to move quickly while on both knees is much more difficult. In addition to this crew member, several other members on the incident were seen in a similar posture with both knees on the ground. If the crew member had been on only one knee, they may have been able to move when they saw/felt the car shifting. The scope would be considered Pattern because there was a concentrated pattern of behavior where several members had two knees down, but is not Widespread as the department teaches the one knee down method. The risk is critical as it is directly linked to preventing a safety incident and is therefore High Risk.

- The injured crew member was wearing gloves they typically use to rack hose, not the padded and reinforced extrication gloves provided. Had the crew member been wearing the proper PPE, the fingers may have been only bruised instead of lacerated. Not wearing the proper PPE is a risky action, however the crew member was wearing a minimum level of protection against hand abrasions. Therefore, the risk level would be Moderate Risk in this case. This is Limited in scope because the injured crew member was the only one wearing the incorrect gloves.

- The department has not focused any of their drills recently on vehicle extrication. While this may have contributed indirectly, it was not the direct cause of why the incident happened. Because of this the level is Low Risk, with a

Widespread scope as it pertains to the entire department drilling schedule.

Figure 15. SAFER Matrix – Vehicle Extrication Example

SAFER Matrix

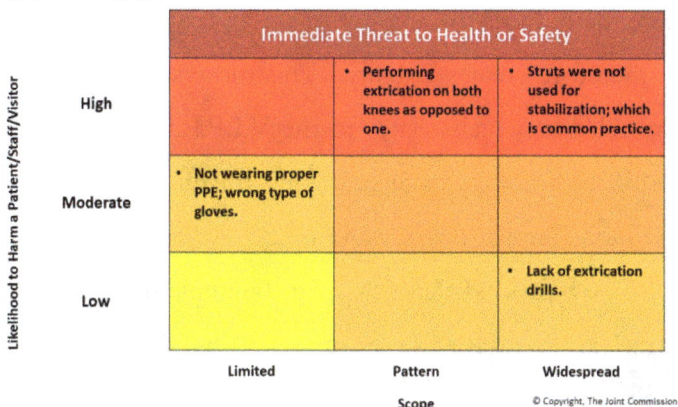

© Joint Commission Resources. (SAFER Matrix Infographic). Oakbrook Terrace, Il: Joint Commission on Accreditation of Healthcare Organizations, (2023), (p. 1). Reprinted with permission.

Figure 15 shows the risks identified plotted to the corresponding place on the matrix. Using this method, it is easy to see the highest priority items that need to be addressed. It also provides all the information in an organized graphic for both quick and comprehensive understanding. The department would focus first on addressing the top two red box items, working from right to left. After these are addressed, the light orange items would be the subject of focus next in descending order.

Chapter Summary

Within the V.I.P.E.R. Improvement Model, the risk assessment quality of the FMEA and SAFER Matrix both relate to the Variance Inhibiting value. The process of managing risk inherently reduces the amount of variance a process might endure, and therefore creates stability. This more stable process makes it more reliable, which relates to the V.I.P.E.R. value of Reliability. The FMEA has a forward-thinking posture that can be used in continuous improvement of a process that is already implemented or in a new process that has yet to be implemented. The SAFER Matrix has a responsive posture that is able to aggregate and prioritize various risks or failures that have occurred to help focus attention.

Conclusion

Now that you have made it through the book and the V.I.P.E.R. Improvement Model, let's go back to the example we started with at the beginning. You are sitting at a meeting and have been asked what to do? Well, now that you have learned the V.I.P.E.R. Improvement Model, you can use it to work through the problem. Now you can give an answer like this, "Well, I think these are all issues that need to be addressed. But first I think we need to figure out where our priorities are so we can work through these things the right way. I think we should spend the next meeting or two creating a strategic plan with a mission, vision, values, S.M.A.R.T. goals, SWOT, and a balanced scorecard. This way we can prioritize our efforts. Then we can measure and track these things using control charts to judge our performance, and once we identify where we are underperforming use either a pareto chart, fishbone diagram, or the 5 Why's tool to investigate the root causes to these issues. If we find that some of these issues are outward facing, let's put together a marketing plan using the 5P's and 5C's, and if they are inward facing let's use strategic human resource management and motivation-based tactics. Once we come up with our solutions, let's use the B.U.R.N. Change Management Model to implement them, and then use either an FMEA or SAFER Matrix to see where our risks are." As you can see, this is a very systematic and purposeful way to address the problem you are faced with. Not only does this allow others to have confidence in you as a leader because you have a thoughtful plan, but it also allows the tools to provide other perspectives and solutions that you as an individual might not have thought of. In reality you shouldn't be expected to have all the answers, but as a leader you do need to know how to find them. That is what the V.I.P.E.R. Improvement Model provides, a way to tackle problems and uncover solutions.

The examples in this book aren't an endorsement of a specific solution necessarily, they are simply given to help the reader understand the concepts. Also, keep in mind that utilization of these techniques may be met with some resistance at your department (see the change management chapter for elaboration as to why). Essentially, change requires new work to be done that is unfamiliar. Some people may not want to roll up their sleeves or are comfortable in the way things currently are. You will need to spend some time explaining what the problem is, why it's important to fix, and explain how these tools can help. Be persistent. These tools and techniques are backed by proven quality improvement science and have been used in many other industries for quite some time. This book isn't based on one person's opinion regarding how a fire department should be run, it's based on improvement methodologies leveraged in sectors such as manufacturing, transportation, and healthcare.

Too many times we have been lectured or have seen the catchy yet hollow social media posts regarding fire department leadership. If you listen closely, the insights that are given are the personal gripes of that person to reinforce their own ego. They seldom give you the tools to make a difference, to make a plan, to fix an issue. This book explains the issues, explains *why* they are issues to provide understanding, and most importantly, gives proven tools and techniques to help you manage and facilitate change. This was the prime reason that provided motivation for me to write this book. It's a disservice to fire and EMS departments that we haven't been provided these types of tools that other industries have been using for decades. Well, that problem has been remedied. Use these tools to make a difference. Beware, you may experience pushback initially. This apprehension is due to the fact that these tools cut through the excuses, add clarity, and drive accountability which will be uncomfortable for those that aren't familiar with such efficiency and effectiveness. Persevere. Find change agents to promote your efforts when you aren't around and gain the support of those you report up to in order to gain the support you need.

Again, real problems need real solutions. The only way to connect these two elements is through tried and proven quality improvement techniques. Hence the V.I.P.E.R. Improvement Model.

References

Bittel, L. (1972). *The Nine Master Keys of Management*. McGraw-Hill. ISBN: 0070054762

Duncan, A. (1974). *Quality Control and Industrial Statistics*. Richard D. Irwin, Inc. ISBN: 0256015589

Fahy, R., Evarts, B., & Stein, G. (2022). NFPA report—U.S. Fire Department Profile. https://www.nfpa.org/News-and-Research/Data-research-and-tools/Emergency-Responders/US-fire-department-profile

Pynes, J., & Lombardi, D. N. (2012). *Human resources management for health care organizations: A strategic approach* (1st ed.). ISBN: 9786613409591

Risk Analysis and Risk Management. (2023). MindTools. https://www.mindtools.com/abhkwcn/risk-analysis-and-risk-management

About the Author

Dr. David Hupp has been a volunteer firefighter/EMT for over a decade with increasing roles and responsibilities as an officer both operationally and administratively. Dr. Hupp is a *Firehouse Magazine* published author, and works as a Quality Improvement professional at the Johns Hopkins Hospital where he uses many of the tools identified in this book daily. Dr. Hupp received his Doctorate in Business Administration – Healthcare Management from Liberty University, and lives in Calvert County, MD with his wife and children.

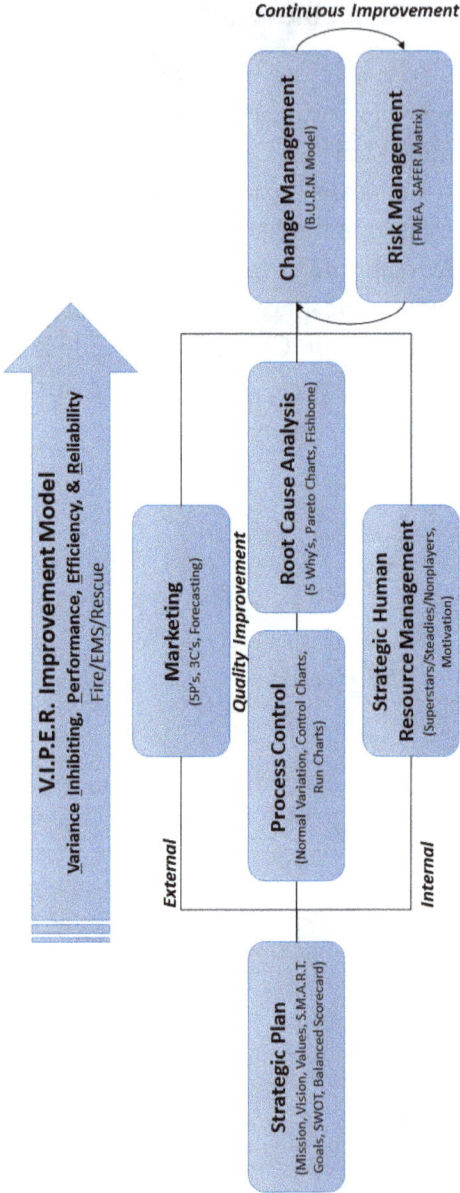

V.I.P.E.R. Improvement Model

Variance Inhibiting, Performance, Efficiency, & Reliability
Fire/EMS/Rescue

Continuous Improvement

Change Management
(B.U.R.N. Model)

Risk Management
(FMEA, SAFER Matrix)

Marketing
(5P's, 3C's, Forecasting)

Root Cause Analysis
(5 Why's, Pareto Charts, Fishbone)

Process Control
(Normal Variation, Control Charts, Run Charts)

Strategic Human Resource Management
(Superstars/Steadies/Nonplayers, Motivation)

Strategic Plan
(Mission, Vision, Values, S.M.A.R.T. Goals, SWOT, Balanced Scorecard)

Quality Improvement

External

Internal

www.ingramcontent.com/pod-product-compliance
Lightning Source LLC
Chambersburg PA
CBHW061258220326
41599CB00028B/5702